D0629513

Fat Chicks
Float Well

Fat Chicks Float Well

≈

the journey toward self-acceptance can be fun
when you discover the special gift of buoyancy

Kate Cronin Haslach

ZOTTY PRESS

Editor: Helen Kimmelfield
Cover Illustration and Design: Rebecca Molayem
Page and Jacket Design: Anita Jones, Another Jones Graphics
Back cover photograph: Michole Jensen

Library of Congress Control Number: 2009928868

ISBN: 978-0-615-28654-9

First Edition

Zotty Press
2065 NW Miller Road, #206
Portland, OR 97229

Printed in the USA

To my fellow travelers,
may you belly-flop with open arms
through this journey called life

Contents

Foreword

≈

The first time I met Kathryn Cronin was in the sleepy beach town of Gearhart on the Oregon coast in 1984. She was a pastry chef at 'Eat Your Heart Out', a wonderful, stylish café popular with the Portland summer crowd thronging to that part of the coast every summer. Her cheeks were rosy, and the twinkle in her eye was testimony to her Irish heritage. I watched her in her chef's whites, as she conversed without interrupting her task of kneading the buttery croissant dough for which the bakery was famous. That first impression of Kathryn was indelible: I can still picture her, making polite conversation as her twinkle turned to a tenacious focus on the dough, and flour puffed in clouds at the mercy of her strong arms.

I have known Kathryn's family since I was being courted by my husband-to-be in the late seventies. Kathryn Leadbetter Cronin is the descendent of a famous Oregon pioneer family, the great-great-grand-daughter of the then owner of *The Oregonian*.

Her grandmother, 104 years old at this writing, is a Leadbetter, whose family history is rooted in the gentrification of Portland in the swaggering boom years of fishing and logging at the turn of the twentieth century.

Eight years after that first meeting, I received a phone call from Kathryn, who was then living in the Bay area. Kathryn's voice is distinctive and sweet, her manner refined, but direct. She wanted to swim the English Channel, she said, and she wanted me to be her mentor. I had only recently resigned from my family business to care for our three children. My youngest was two. I remember feeling the blood rush to my head; memories of my own attempt to swim the English Channel on August 4, 1979, washed over me like an icy wave. I had battled frigid temperatures, relentless tides, and jellyfish in the busiest shipping channel in the world. And I had lost. After 11 ½ hours in the water, I was 2 ½ miles off the shore of France when I hit the outgoing tide and swam in place for two hours before my coach leaned over the side of the old fishing-boat and tapped me on the head, resulting in an automatic disqualification. Contact during an official swim, human or artificial, means the swim is over. This is just one of a long list of strict rules and guidelines laid down by the English Channel Swimming Association, the governing body for all official swims.

For Kathryn I was hopeful, but I was also fearful. I knew what was at stake, and what the odds were: only five percent of those who attempt to swim across the English Channel are successful. It is the ultimate test of speed and endurance for open-water swimmers.

One month later on a crisp, spring morning in 1992, I was at Lake Sonoma in Northern California, sitting in a small outboard cruising boat, more like a party barge, with five friends from the famous Dolphin Club in San Francisco. We were there to support Kathryn as she prepared for an endurance swim under conditions mimicking those in the Channel. It was very chilly: the water in the lake was actually too cold, 57°F at dawn. The air temperature was 38°F, with a brisk 15 m.p.h. wind. The water temperature in the Channel is 59-60°F. I knew that a ten-hour swim would be a challenge in those temperatures. The difference between 57 and 60 degrees is huge, when it comes to hypothermia and human physiology. And then I watched this 31-year-old woman; I timed her strokes in the impossibly cold water and air. She was in absolutely peak condition. She swam with sheer grit and true ability for six and a quarter hours. I knew then that she had what it would take to conquer the English Channel. A month later, she went back to the same lake and easily swam in 60 degrees for ten hours. It was a real honor to help train such a swimmer to scale the Mt. Everest of open-water swims.

The night before the Sonoma swim, Kathryn informed me that we were going swimming in the San Francisco Bay. I was 36 years old, and had done no open-water swimming since being pulled from the Channel thirteen years before. I was a marathon runner, and had long since shed the twenty pounds I had gained in order to endure the cold of the Channel. Kathryn's unshakeable optimism gave me the confidence to tiptoe into the Bay that moonlit April night. We swam, adrenaline flowing, gasping for breath in the frigid water, straight towards the Golden Gate Bridge. It was an incredibly redeeming and liberating experience for me. For the first time in a long time I felt free from my self-imposed shackles. I remember looking over at Kathryn as we stopped and trod water in the middle of the Bay. We could see the glowing lights of Fisherman's Wharf and the Golden Gate Bridge against a pink sunset, as the moon rose over Alcatraz. There were people going about their everyday business on the Wharf and there we were, giddy with a touch of hypothermia, taking it all in, a couple of voyeurs looking at life from a unique perspective. Kathryn gave me a knowing look as she said, "I knew you would love this." Was she right!

Kathryn pulled me out of a life that was a little mundane and predictable, to face an old failure and take a step toward confronting the challenges that had defeated me thirteen years before. I only knew that at that very moment, it was the right thing to do. No hesitation. Kathryn had known it all along!

Winning in the end is not about the sweet bliss of victory. The real lessons we learn in life are what we learn from our failures. And sometimes we have to learn the lessons over and over before we 'get it'. In this autobiography, Kathryn reveals her flaws and her fears, her imperfect, but *what-is-perfect?* search for her own truths. She bravely exposes the demons she is battling. She reaches a point of acceptance. And she teaches us all the coping techniques she has developed along the way. This story is written with love, about love, and forgiveness: love, in its grace and ferocity, in the unconditional support of our families and our friends; forgiveness, of oneself and others as we, and they, strive to do better; the stuff of life that keeps us going every day.

Kathryn and I live in the same town. We talk occasionally. We are friends but we don't hang out together on a regular basis. We are connected on a different level. I know I could huddle on a boat in the cold for hours, watching her swim, and knowing that when she took a breath she would see that I was there. And I know she would do the same for me. Kathryn kneads and punches away at life, just as she was working that dough the day we met, kneading and punching until it is molded into something satisfying and nourishing. *Fat Chicks Float Well* opens a window onto Kathryn's personal journey. Her story reflects the travails and tears of a generation that came of age in the sixties and seventies: our passions, our goals, our triumphs and our defeats. The only thing I find myself wanting from this story is more! Kathryn followed me into the Channel; I look forward to following her through the next phase of her life. Meanwhile, I feel privileged to have been in a couple of chapters along the way.

Gail Bowen McCormick

Introduction

≈

Gail taught herself to speak backwards during her swim. Maybe I'll try that. N-Y-R-H-T-A-K, "Nearhitack". R-E-T-T-E-B-D-E-A-L, "Rettebdeal". That was easier. N-I-N-O-R-C, sounds Eskimoish. My name is Nyrhtak Rettibdeal Ninorc! Whichever side of the brain that comes from, I don't have it. I'm stuck inside myself for the next twelve plus hours. My silicone ear plugs are jammed inside my ears so deep, I can hear my heart beat. My shoulders, underarms, and upper legs are smothered in "Channel Grease", my goggles so hazy I feel I'm going to have to reach outside myself to see where I am. I taste gritty brackish water, but my body has good circulation in this 61°F stretch of ocean, better known as the English Channel.

Suddenly, Mic, my new Irish friend, leans over the rail of the thirty-foot fishing boat with my dry-erase board. 5 MIN. Yay! In five minutes I get to scull the water for twelve seconds while I get a mouthful of banana and chug four ounces of heated electrolytes, which I prepared and poured into my gallon thermos at 3:45 this morning. Life just doesn't get any better than this!

Twenty minutes later, my bladder reaches full capacity. Holding it in is beginning to drain my energy. I swim breaststroke so that I can relax my tight groin muscles enough to relieve myself. The warm liquid surrounding my legs brings much needed comfort to my cramped core. I go back to swimming the crawl stroke. I watch the blue and white boat over my right shoulder.

Mike, the captain of the off-season fishing vessel, leans over the port side of the boat and yells "We're auf way coffee". I stop swimming and try to read his lips. Do I waste the energy to correct him? "My name is not Kathy. You can call me Kate or Kathryn". I don't think so.

I realize what he said. "We're half way!" I emerge from the fog that has settled on my brain. The water is like glass. I can see my arms cutting through the top surface of the ocean. My stroke rate is steady at 72 counts per minute and I can see FRANCE. Mic writes on the dry-erase board: 5 HR, 12 MIN. I am way ahead of schedule. If I can maintain this pace, I'll have swum the English Channel in ten hours and twenty-four minutes. Cool. Little did I know that this was the proverbial calm before the storm. I certainly didn't know then that I would later describe my English Channel experience as an epiphany, a defining moment in my life which would guide me for years to come, a realization like many, filled with complexities, contradictions, and challenges.

So what was my epiphany? Very simple. You've heard it before, I'm sure. Simply put, I found myself on a journey toward self-acceptance. What I didn't realize, though, was that this journey would never end. For me and for millions of others, getting to self-acceptance is a life-long trip, with lots of side roads and sometimes very unpleasant minefields. Self-acceptance may be relatively easy to spell, and easy to say, but it's very tricky to achieve unconditionally.

My goal in writing this book is to shatter the isolation experienced by beautiful but imperfect people attempting to "fit in" some place in this universe. My own "imperfection" is 200 pounds on a 5'4" frame. Trying to understand how I got to this weight, I learned that we need to work with what we are and, most of all, have fun being ourselves. Life, as it is this very minute, is a precious gift. We cannot waste another day worrying about what other people think of us. In my personal journey toward self-acceptance, I discovered that buoyancy is a very special gift. I am thrilled to share my journey and that gift with you.

What special gift of your own would you like to share with family and friends?

Do you worry about what people think of you? Does it serve you well to do so, or is it a waste of time?

No-one is perfect. Accepting this fact is the first step towards a happy life. What imperfection of your own stands in the way of your personal progress?

"The purpose of life is a life of purpose."
—Robert Byrne

Growing Up Kathryn

Who I Am Today

Before I get started on my journey toward self-acceptance, I thought I'd let you know who I am today. I'm a forty-eight-year-old, married white woman, mother of two teenagers, gourmet cook, an entrepreneur, a water loving, ex-competitive swimmer, and, in Natural Horsemanship terms (more on Natural Horsemanship later), a left brain extrovert: playful, naughty, mischievous, willful, exuberant and friendly. Currently, I have two children, two cats, two goldfish, two horses and only one husband...thank God.

Now, this book is about a lot more than food and my weight, but since they've both taught me so much and are very much a part of my journey, I figure I'd better lay them out right here. The fact is, it's hard to discuss my weight with people because I don't feel as if I'm fifty pounds over my ideal number. I feel fit and strong and I increasingly enjoy the feelings I have about myself. I am learning to love myself as if I were my daughter. I praise my fourteen-year-old for her efforts in sports, grades and friendships. I am learning to do the same for myself.

GarBinge Eating

I'm learning, but I'm still traveling. Like many other food addicts, I overeat to escape a sense of pressure of frustration, a habit which, to my chagrin, has found a welcome home somewhere in my subconscious. The fact is that, instead of turning to alcohol or drugs, I've medicated myself with food and, as do medications in general, mine have their own predictable routines.

One routine in particular is unfailingly set in motion when I'm playing Spider Solitaire on the computer—one of my favorite ways to escape the pressures of everyday life. It goes like this: Spider Solitaire; eat, deal, play; eat, deal, play. My conscious brain has coined the term "GarBinge eating" to describe what it sees when the other part of me is dominant. To keep that "other" part of me somewhat in check, I now keep a bag of apricots by the computer, so that when I reach, it won't be for junk food.

I also set myself a time limit on my computer game. It's still an escape for me and allows my thoughts to settle when I'm upset about something, or noodling over new ideas. It gives me a "time out," a kind of psychic space that allows my mood to transition from frustration to peace and calm.

There's more than a bit of irony in all this, I know. I've always been a gifted cook, and, since my English Channel Swim, it gives me great pleasure to prepare wonderful meals for my family and friends. My brain is already wired to connect food with love. I need my brain to go one step further, to connect *me* with unconditional love for myself. My journey toward self-acceptance continues. Where are you on yours?

MY CHILDHOOD

I grew up in a *traditional* dysfunctional Irish Catholic family. My father did the drinking and my mother did the guilt trips. As a teen-ager, I could always tell when my mother was upset with me. She would "accidentally on purpose" put egg shells in my scrambled eggs. I'm one of six children: three girls and three boys. I was *Cindy* of the Brady Bunch. All of us children grew up learning to cope with the family dynamic in different ways, many of which were unhealthy. For most people, life is one long lesson in retraining ourselves. What I have discovered in writing this book is how I learned to float around my particular obstacles.

When I was very young, my mother taught me to go only by the name "Kathryn." Whenever someone called me Kathy, I would respond, dutifully "My name is Kathryn, *not* Kathy." Looking back and seeing all the mischief I got into, I realize there was yet another person in me, pushing her way out. "Kate" is her name, and she ached to release the free spirit cooped up within me for so long.

It wasn't until I moved to San Francisco in 1991, that I released Kate from her cage, and filed Kathryn under "conventional." Not to worry. I'm not schizophrenic. There had just finally come a time in my life when I realized that I liked who I was, and had the confidence not to worry about pleasing others. I also learned that if I followed my heart, doors would open.

Aging Naturally

Today, I value living and aging naturally, and have no intention of hiding my gray hair or the wrinkles that will come with time. My conscious brain has a mantra, actually, a whole series of mantras: "I am who I am; I needn't keep up with the Joneses or my sisters; I'm happy being me; I'm secure with myself; I needn't worry about others' judgments; I have to live up to *my* standards, no one else's."

My mantras continue: "I value being non-judgmental towards other people; it will be something I strive for throughout my life. I value honesty in myself; I wish it of others, but I am not in charge of them."

Okay. I said my *conscious* brain has the mantras. Obviously, it still gets competition for attention from that pesky other part, but my conscious brain is the one I'm listening to today.

When I lived in Napa Valley in my late twenties, I was never alone because I was with myself. However, now that I'm so busy with my everyday tasks I'm sometimes lonely for the other person I was meant to be, the woman who will pursue my other dreams. I know that I'm a country girl at heart, living the hectic lifestyle of a city person, satisfying my family's needs.

Skin Cancer *In*

Now that I'm in the "August" of my life, my coco-butter upbringing of the 1960's and the sun exposure from open-water swimming has caught up with me. Recently diagnosed with basal cell carcinoma on my face, I am thankful it's not melanoma. I faced my fears and had the grueling three-hour Mohs Procedure on my cheek, on January 2, 2009; what a way to start the year. Scars add character, and boy do I have character, all over my body. I am just a tapestry of scars from my ACL knee surgery, two C-sections, an appendectomy, several breast biopsies, and now, my face! Besides, if I ever pose for Playboy, they can airbrush the pictures. Not even.

I called my mom in California, last December, on the day I got my diagnosis. I explained that I had the Portland Garden Club Market Basket Preview Party that evening and a bandage on my face from the biopsy that morning. My mom, a thirty-four-year veteran of the Garden Club, matter-of-factly declared "Why band-aids *are in* at the Garden Club. *Everyone* has them!" I had to laugh. I am so in style.

Describe the person you are today, in terms of work, play, family, and personality.

Identify habitual behaviors that you engage in, either consciously or subconsciously.

If you haven't done so already, create personal mantras that reflect your positive beliefs and aims.

"Most people are about as happy as they make up their minds to be."

—Abraham Lincoln

A Fish Out of Water 2

THE LOVE BOAT SANK

I moved to Santa Monica in the fall of 1988 to escape what had become an emotionally unhealthy environment in Portland. I realized I needed to sever the damaged relationships I had with my father and sister in order to allow my healing process to begin. Six months before my move, I'd interviewed with Citmar Cruises in Los Angeles, hoping for a Social Director position. They told me to get back in touch in six months. I don't think they meant for me to actually move blindly to California but at the time, it was the obvious decision. Shortly after my arrival I called Citmar headquarters from Santa Monica, only to find that the cruise line had been bought out by Princess Cruises and the job I'd wanted wasn't going to materialize.

LA LA LAND

With no job in sight and my finances dwindling fast, I had luck on my side when I was able to move into an apartment with two UCLA nurses I'd met briefly during a trip to Sun Valley. Even though I had a roof over my head, I readied my coveted coin collection for the chopping block and then, knowing that the proceeds from my collection weren't going to be enough to support me, I made my way to Borders and purchased a book on the best companies to work for in the Los Angeles area.

In 1985 I received my Bachelor's degree in Hotel, Restaurant and Tourism Management from Oregon State, but I wanted to venture outside of the hospitality industry. After reading my new book, researching companies in the area, I managed to finagle an interview with Chiat/Day Advertising Agency in Venice Beach, but when I showed up for the second interview, the manager remarked to me that she had mistaken me for someone else. Were they looking at my resume, or my silhouette? They offered me a job as a receptionist for a mere sixteen thousand dollars a year. I decided to keep looking.

GAINFUL EMPLOYMENT

I ended up with two jobs, both safely within my comfort zone. In the mornings I walked nine blocks to Montana Mercantile, on the posh aptly named Montana Avenue, where they sold gourmet kitchen equipment and maintained a demonstration kitchen for cooking classes. My job was to prepare all those neatly arranged little ramekin dishes with the two tablespoons of minced garlic, the half teaspoon cumin, etc. By the time the Chef arrived and cooking classes started, every ingredient was lined up as if by magic! It was here that I first met Hugh Carpenter, the famous Celebrity Chef. Later I would attend Hugh's Camp Napa cooking classes and garden tours with my Mother when we celebrated my 40th birthday.

After putting in long days at Montana Mercantile, I would walk home, take a shower, change into a dress and drive to a trendy Mediterranean restaurant called Opera, across from the famous Santa Monica pier. There I worked the dinner shift as hostess, greeting the many celebrities as they walked through the door. Being a naïve Oregonian, I had to literally push my jaw up when the likes of Sally Field, Quincy Jones, or Jeff Bridges entered the restaurant. Ali MacGraw called to make New Year's Day brunch reservations for her family. When I asked her if she needed a highchair for her son, she laughed, saying she loved me, because her baby boy was now in his twenties! I kept a notepad with the names of all the celebrities who entered the restaurant. When I showed it to the manager, he laughed heartily. Only an Oregonian would do such a thing in Los Angeles.

I guess "Oregon" showed all over me because I was forever getting asked, "Where are you from?" I responded by asking how they knew I was not a native. All said the same thing: I smiled too much. Oh well, maybe I really did look like a dumb Oregonian, but at least I was still smiling.

THE LOVE CONNECTION

On my rare day off I would crash in front of the television. One fun thing unique to Southern California, the hub of game shows, was that local residents were always being invited to participate in those programs. After watching *The Love Connection*, hosted by Chuck Woolery, I heard a voice-over say, "If you would like to be on the Love Connection, please call this number to make a video." There again, being a naïve Oregonian, I called the telephone number and made an appointment to go to their studio to make the video.

One thing *The Love Connection* producer explained to me before making the video was that the game show was for entertainment purposes, and that I needed to captivate the audience. Ok. Desperate times call for desperate measures. The Kate in me came to the rescue. In my video I explained that I was *Betty Crocker of the '90's* and that the fastest way to a man's heart was through his stomach. Original, ha? I also described my ideal first date taking place on a tennis court. That way I could sieve out the schleps right there and then.

WISE ADVICE
It didn't take very long before I found the materialistic Southern Californian lifestyle too superficial for me; I needed an environment that allowed me to be authentic. I discussed my life-plan options with my step-father, Jack, and told him I'd always wanted to live in Napa Valley. During my senior year at Oregon State, I went on a field trip to Tahoe, UC Davis, and Napa Valley. Sitting in the back of the bus, I thought, "Someday soon, I need to live in Napa Valley."

"It's easy, just get in your car and GO", Jack declared. Taking his advice literally, I gave notice to both employers.

After six months in Santa Monica I'd come to the conclusion that I would not thrive in an environment where I didn't want to fit in. Living there, I felt like a fish out of water cast up on dry asphalt, gasping for oxygen. For the first time in my life I followed my heart, north to Napa Valley.

THE NAPA VALLEY DATE

As luck would have it, the very *day* I left Los Angeles, in the spring of 1989, I heard from *The Love Connection*. My friend Deb, who lived in San Francisco, had driven down to Santa Monica to help me with my move. I settled into her small, bay-windowed apartment in San Francisco while I looked for a place to hang up my hat in Napa Valley. It was then time to call home to let my mom know that I had survived the monotonous drive through the San Joaquin Valley. No sooner had I gotten Mother on the phone when my sister grabbed the receiver and told me *The Love Connection* had called and said the guy had chosen me for his date. I declared my sister full of shit and was about to hang up when Sara said that Amy, the producer, had called and here was her phone number! I had to laugh at the irony.

Assuming it would be far too late for a date; I decided "What the heck!" and dialed the one-eight hundred number my sister gave me. I got directly through to the show's producer, who suggested that my date, Paul, drive up to the Bay area and that we could go on our date up there. She asked if I were up for it. Again, I thought, "What the heck."

It took a week for Paul to organize his trip up north. By then I had a deposit on a cute little cottage I'd discovered in Calistoga, but I returned to Deb's apartment for my date. I was nervous about meeting a total stranger, and on top of that was the pressure of having to *entertain* the audience. I needed to keep the mischievous Kate at bay! Knowing that he would not be able to make the date a day trip, I asked Paul to bring a sleeping bag along.

Our date started off with a trolley-car ride to Fisherman's Wharf, where we blended in with the hundreds of other tourists. Lunch was on *The Love Connection's* padded wallet. We then took Paul's rental car up to Napa Valley for a wine tasting at the beautiful Mondavi Vineyards, the premier winery that put Napa Valley on the map.

Afterwards, we had a nice romantic fireside dinner at the Calistoga Inn, but sparks weren't flying and I knew it wouldn't be worth sleeping with him just to get on the show, nor was I going to create a Jerry Springer knock-down, drag-out fight just to please the audience. I'd left the superficial living five hundred miles south.

That night Paul slept on the floor of my unfurnished living room and I in my sleeping bag on the bedroom floor. On our way back to the city, we didn't make plans for a second date. Shortly afterwards, Amy called and tried to squeeze every detail from me about our date, but came up dry. My *Love Connection* debut may have failed, but my heart quivered at the prospect of fulfilling my dream of living in Napa Valley. On my drive back north to my new home, I rolled down my car window, inhaling the sweet scent of mustard flowers and cried tears of joy!

Have you ever made a decision or taken action based solely on following your heart?

At a certain points in my life, I have understood that something had to change, either myself or my environment. Has this ever happened to you? What did you do about it?

"I shall return."

—Douglas MacArthur,
after leaving the Philippines, March 1942

NV Dreaming 3

Moving to Napa Valley was a dream come true. I loved every-thing about the area. It was fun to explore the valley by foot, mountain bike and by car. Deep down, I've always been a country bumpkin. I was thrilled to be living in a small community and looked forward to meeting as many people as possible.

GARDEN THERAPY

The minute I laid eyes on the cute little cottage in Calistoga, I knew I'd found my home. The existing garden was a shambles, and I couldn't wait to unlock my own secret garden. Since I hadn't taken my cat, *Boo,* and my furniture to Santa Monica, I drove back up to Portland, loaded them up, and took them to my new home. On arrival, I immediately attacked the garden surrounding my cottage. This was my very first garden and I couldn't wait to see the neglected plants brought to their full potential.

As my surroundings began to take shape, I realized that the physical exercise of gardening was an excellent way to release emotional tension buried deep down from childhood. While pruning and fertilizing the rose garden alongside my cottage, I thought of the many thorns that had poked my own past, letting them drift in front of my face like a bubble, then pop in mid-air. Behind the cottage, a bed of irises that badly needed dividing was pulled apart, the soil tilled and amended and the tubers replanted. I was quickly rewarded with a bed of tall and sturdy purple bearded Iris. Like the iris, I could feel my feet starting to grow their own roots.

I was thrilled to discover right in front of the cottage, hidden under overgrown brush and trees, a beautiful built-in stone barbecue. I knew that after I had brought this area to life, it would become a favorite spot where I would entertain my new friends and enjoy the sweet evening fragrances unique to the Napa Valley.

BERINGER SCHOOL FOR AMERICAN CHEFS

After three weeks of playing in my garden, I decided it was time to look for a job. I pulled out a map of the valley and drew a circle around ten of the wineries where I would drop off my culinary resume. At least I had a plan. I knew that Knickerbocker's restaurant had an outstanding catering service, so I decided to lunch there and see them in action. After lunch I met with the catering manager and showed him my resume. To my amazement and delight, he was looking for a Catering Manager and thought I would fit the bill. My fifteen years in the catering field would finally pay off! He also suggested that I visit Beringer Vineyards, as Madeleine Kamman, a famous French cookbook author and chef, was developing the School for American Chefs and their first session would be starting in six weeks.

The signs were too good to ignore; I found my way to the famed Beringer Vineyards. There I knocked on the culinary center's front door and was promptly told to take my resume to the backdoor, where the kitchen was. Again, to my amazement, I was hired on the spot to be a preparation cook. It wasn't a management position, but I was happy to be in close proximity to the new program. Three weeks later, Madeleine fired her new assistant and hired me. Timing was everything.

The brand-new School for American Chefs consisted of six, two-week sessions for top American chefs who had sent in videos of themselves at work and designed a full menu for Madeleine to critique. After being invited to attend the school, these select chefs came to Napa Valley to work with the infamously ill-tempered French chef. Madeleine had been known to shake her knife at students (or me) saying, "What's a Momma to do?" or "You drive me banana!" All things considered, my job proved to be an incredible opportunity for me to meet and work with the crème de la crème of chefs from coast to coast. I bought Madeleine's book, *In Madeleine's Kitchen* and asked each chef to sign it. I cherished their sweet remarks and invitations to visit them at their restaurants.

While the chefs prepared outstanding five-course dinners for the elite vineyard community, I fed them breakfast, lunch and dinner. Talk about pressure! However, one of my menu items was a particular hit. It was none other than a special German Pancake recipe, the ingredients of which I had perfectly refined, resulting in a delicious, buttery, golden trough. They all insisted I share the recipe with them, and permit them to take it back to their own restaurants. Since these illustrious chefs were from every corner of the United States, my recipe and I are probably famous, and I don't even know it! I was touched and honored to share it with them then, and with you now!

Kate's German Pancake

3 tablespoons butter

1 cup all-purpose flour
¼ cup sugar
1/2 teaspoon salt

1 cup milk, room temperature (microwave for 30 seconds)
1 teaspoon vanilla extract
2 eggs, room temperature (soak in warm water for 5 minutes)

Maple syrup
Lemon wedges
Confectioner's sugar

Preheat oven to 450°F. Place butter in a 9" x 13" Pyrex dish and let butter melt in oven while preheating. Keep an eye on the butter, to make sure it doesn't burn.

Using a wire whisk, stir the dry ingredients in a bowl. Beat together the milk, vanilla and eggs, pour on top of the flour mixture and whisk for 1 minute. Pour batter into the heated glass Pyrex dish with the melted butter and return to the oven. Bake for approximately 12-15 minutes. The edges will rise and turn brown when ready. Have your audience right there, ready to witness the breakfast miracle as it comes out of the oven, because it will fall immediately. Sprinkle powdered sugar over the pancake and serve with lemon wedges and maple syrup. Enjoy!

This recipe makes two large portions or four small portions.

While living in Napa Valley, I mastered this recipe. After Saturday morning swim practice, I'd experiment with the ingredients until I got just the right proportions for a half recipe. Of course, I would then proceed to eat every last bite.

OPENING CLOSED DOORS

Besides having this exciting culinary career, I also found myself getting involved with the community. I joined the Masters swimming team at the community pool next to St. Helena high school. Team swimming introduced me to the salt of the earth, dedicated, hard-working, reliable people who loved the water, like me. We were kindred spirits. I volunteered to chair a fund-raiser for the pool. My swimming buddies and I also walked in Calistoga's hot Fourth of July parade with swim caps and goggles on, inviting everyone to join us in the pool. Afterwards, some friends set up their band in my garden and we partied until the fireworks were burned out.

I was also invited to join a Calistoga coed softball team. Although I was not known for my softball skills, everyone knew I was great at team camaraderie *after* the games. Additionally, I volunteered for the annual Napa Valley Wine Auction, which was the valley's biggest event. This, in turn, allowed me to participate without having to pay thousands of dollars to get a front-row seat; I stood in the front, with a paddle in hand, directing the head auctioneer toward bidders. I was even hired to be an extra on a made-for-television murder mystery movie starring Jacqueline Smith. I played a caterer at the famous Inglenook Vineyards property.

Another of my volunteer jobs was serving as secretary for the Napa Valley Culinary Alliance, where I got to work with well-known foodies, organizing events throughout the valley. I helped prepare food for the spectacular opening celebration of the Culinary Institute of America at Greystone, formerly Christian Brothers Winery. Our meetings took place at wineries and in back yards of private residences that I would have never otherwise experienced. We also gathered to taste Sake, Balsamic vinegar, and sparkling wines. It was the best of times, being poor in paradise and thriving!

The Rhine House Opportunity

As I said before, timing is everything. When Madeleine's camp closed down for the season, I realized I needed a steady job for the rest of the year. Next door to the Culinary Center was the famous Beringer Rhine House, the headquarters for their wine tasting and tours. The manager, Jim, was creating a new position as Rhine House Administrative Coordinator. Taking a big step out of the kitchen, I ventured into the business field to try my hand at the computer keyboard. Jim was beyond patient with me as I learned how to use the computer and Microsoft programs in creating his monthly financial reports. It was an opportunity to learn a whole new industry, away from the kitchen and temperamental chefs, and I came to respect Jim very much as he pushed me to be precise in my work. His patience allowed me to learn new skills that serve me to this day. I continued working at Beringer's Rhine House for the next year and a half.

My swimming also took a new path. Venturing out of the pool as I had from the kitchen, I belly-flopped with open arms into open-water swimming, I participated in Lake Sonoma, Lake Berryessa, Whiskeytown Lake, Coyote Point beach and Santa Cruz Pier swims. I flourished in the open water, far away from chlorinated pools. Little did I know then that open water swimming would lead me to San Francisco and introduce me to a new friend, my long-lost Kate.

What "thorns" in your past poke you when your emotional guard is down?

Are you a city person living in the country or a country person, living in the city? List the ways you make a good life for yourself under those circumstances.

In addition to helping the community, volunteering can open closed doors. Have you ever experienced the benefits of being a volunteer?

"Nothing great in the world has been accomplished without passion."

—Hegel, *Philosophy of History*

Loving Water 4

MY FRIEND, THE WATER

I grew up a competitive swimmer in the chlorinated 50-meter pool of the Multnomah Athletic Club in Portland, Oregon. It was before any respectable swimmer ever thought of using goggles. I remember showing up for seventh-grade Algebra, with such blood-shot eyes from morning work-outs, I could barely read the chalk board. I'm surprised I wasn't called to the Principal's office for a drug test.

I continued to swim nearly every day until high school, when I discovered tennis, soccer, skiing, and boys. Realizing that competitive swimming would require total commitment, total dedication, I opted for *fun*. Serious swimming would wait a few years until, in an effort to escape the pressures of college life at Oregon State, I joined the swim team. This time, I trained with goggles and although I didn't know it then, my English Channel swim was in the making.

Swimming at college level brought a discipline to my life that I had never before experienced. Though it was tough getting up at 4:30 a.m., lifting weights and swimming for an hour and a half before my first class began, I stuck it out for the whole season and loved getting to know the fellow swimmers. The slowest person in the pool, I was no threat to the other team members. And, since I was twenty-three years old and the other swimmers were between eighteen and twenty, they liked to call me "Grandma."

We can all learn from the different levels of competitive sports. What I learned from my college athletics was that swimming was completely physical, while diving was totally mental. Diving taught me that my brain can control my physical body. I learned I could do anything on the one-meter springboard, as long as I was wearing the thick water-skiing vest!

OPEN-WATER SWIMMING ARRIVES

In 1987, on a lark, I joined a relay team for a triathlon event at Hagg Lake, not far from Portland. I knew instantly that a whole new wet world was opening up for me. I loved swimming in the freshwater environment so far removed from that of chlorinated pools. Open-water swimming was in my blood, and I knew it. Taking every possible opportunity, I found myself leaving behind the cares of the world for the refuge of clear, clean, and very deep waters. One of those opportunities presented itself on Labor Day.

*In the striped swim suit, my first Open-Water event
at Hagg Lake in 1987.*

THE SEED IS PLANTED

I'd joined a couple of friends for the annual Labor Day "Swim Across the Columbia River." I'd never experienced so much fun, jumping off a sternwheeler, feeling as if I were soaring across the river with the current. It was exhilarating!

After our swim in the Columbia River Gorge, my friends and I decided to try wind- surfing. Much harder than it looks, wind-surfing takes incredible strength and balance. On our drive back to Portland, one of my friends, Joe, told me he would like some day to swim the English Channel. The possibility of such a feat had never even occurred to me.

However, as I look back now, I remember as a young child seeing old footage from the movie, *Swim, Girl Swim*. In 1926

Gertrude Ederle was the first woman to swim across the English Channel. In the movie she portrayed herself, all greased-up, swimming to shore near the White Cliffs of Dover.

Unintentional Preparation

A couple of years after my exposure to open-water swimming, I found myself living in Napa Valley, eighty-five miles north of the Bay Area. I started traveling to various open-water events. When I registered for the Santa Cruz Rough-Water Swim, I actually had to have my boss Jim, from Beringer Vineyards, sign my application as a witness. I was informed on the application that the waters were shark-infested due to all the sea lions living under the pier. I had never experienced any type of fear in the water before. The thought of swimming in such dangerous conditions actually boosted my heart rate.

It was with a mixture of excitement and trepidation that I drove down to Santa Cruz with a few fellow swimmers. The swim itself would be a piece of cake, assuming I didn't become one for the sharks. As I swam along side the pier I could see and hear the sea lions packed together under the wood structure, but I felt safe with my own school of swimmers around me.

Soon after the swim, I realized I was going to experience the Santa Cruz party-scene. There was a bunch of rowdy swimmers on the beach, with a keg of beer buried in the sand. One of my friends knew them, so we ventured over.

The Dolphin Club

That day on the Santa Cruz beach was my unexpected introduction to San Francisco's venerable Dolphin Swimming and Rowing Club. They all looked as though they enjoyed life to its fullest, and didn't mind some good-humored bucking of the rules. In order to get a ten-minute start on his appropriate age-group, for example, one of the Dolphin swimmers had actually worn two different-colored swim-caps for the race, one on top of the other. Half-way through the swim, he peeled of the top cap. I thought it hilarious when he got up to receive the trophy for the fastest time. I felt a surprising kindred connection with the Dolphin Club members!

LIFE-CHANGING GOAL

A few months later I saw an Anthony Robbins infomercial. The cassette and book program looked so empowering that I immediately got on the phone and ordered my life-changing guide. When the tapes arrived, I immersed myself in them, sitting in my car at lunch-time, filling out the workbooks, and listening to the empowerment guru. I needed a life-goal, one I could look back on with satisfaction, sitting in my rocking chair at eighty-two years old, a goal that I would never regret. I decided right there and then, sitting in my Nissan Pulsar in the Beringer Vineyards employee parking lot, that I was going to swim the English Channel, while I was young and single, and had the time to dedicate to, what I knew would be a rigid training schedule. That evening I swam for an hour and forty-five minutes at the Calistoga Spa, trying to harness my energy, and focus on what I needed to do next.

One of the most difficult things I ever did in my life was to leave my job at Beringer Vineyards, and Napa Valley. My boss, Jim, had to practically carry me out to my car. Even though I was so distraught at leaving my secure job and cute cottage in Calistoga, I knew that I was taking the right path! I was following my heart and knew it wouldn't lead me astray. I spent exactly two years living in Napa Valley; arriving in Calistoga on March 11, 1989 and moving away on March 11, 1991.

My first act was to join the Dolphin Club in San Francisco, so confident in my decision that, for the first time in my life, I changed my name from Kathryn to Kate. No-one I was about to meet in San Francisco would know me as anything other than Kate.

What are the different names or titles you have gone by at different times in your life? Do you answer to more than one name or title today? How does a particular name or title affect your behavior?

What hard decisions have you had to make in your personal and professional life?

Is there a particular sport that you have been involved in for all or most of your life? If not, how have you remained active over the years?

"One can never pay in gratitude; one can only pay 'in kind' somewhere else in life."

—Anne Morrow Lindbergh

The Dolphin Club 5

I took the plunge, literally. Almost before the membership ink was dry, I'd found my way down to the frigid waters of the Bay. The Sierra snow melt, brought the Bay temperatures dipping in the springtime. Now that I'd officially become a Dolphin, I was free to swim in the Bay anytime and I wasn't going to waste a moment. It didn't hurt that I knew there'd be a welcome reward at the end of each outing, in the form of a thawing hot shower and deliciously long sauna.

The First Step is the Hardest

I was warned early on that the Bay tested newcomers for all they were worth. Failing the test would mean one of two things. You either died from a heart attack or simply didn't come back. Like so many important things in life, taking the first step was the hardest, but I was determined to do it. I quickly learned that the safe entry was slow and methodical; I needed to numb my body gradually.

To do this, I waded in carefully, letting my toes, as advance scouts, learn what the rest of my body was about to experience.

When the water approached my knee caps, the infamous "ice cream headache" struck. That was for starters. Next were my kidneys: once they were iced, I could lean forward and start my crawl stroke. It would be another full ten strokes before I could catch my breath.

It didn't take long before my mental and physical preparation for meeting the Bay waters was predictable. My mind and my body knew what to expect. When the water temperature was below 55°F, it would take a mere 15 seconds before I'd feel as if I was being dumped into a tub of scalding hot water. Almost immediately, the stinging sensation moved from burning pain to nothing. I was numb.

At this point, I knew that my blood had found its way to my vital organs and was protecting them from hypothermia. My arms and legs no longer belonged to me. I couldn't feel my fingers. My brain had to take over my extremities and tell them to move. My limbs felt like two-by-fours, rowing in the water. I no longer felt cold because I couldn't feel anything. Once my body learned to welcome this unnatural state, it could relax and get on with its purpose, to swim. I found it odd, when the water temperature rose a few degrees above fifty-five, my body wouldn't numb-up and I would remain cold through the duration of my swim.

ENDORPHIN JUNKY

"Relax?" you ask. "How could anyone relax in such a state?" The irony is that what is close to unmitigated self-inflicted torture is totally overcome by endorphins, the body's most powerful protectors in times of stress. Given that endorphins are nothing less than a form of morphine, I should not have been surprised at their power not just to protect my body from pain, but also to deliver an unequalled rush that surged through my body hours after the swim was over. Minutes after exiting the icy waters of the Bay, a tingling sensation would hit me, as if I were bathing in soothing Eucalyptus oil.

No wonder Dolphin Club members seemed so happy. We were always on a high. I had become a cold-water junky!

The white building on the right is the Dolphin Club at Aquatic Park in San Francisco.

THE PATH LESS TRAVELED

The Dolphin Club became a second home for me. For many reasons, it was the perfect place for me to find much-needed support and guidance for my cold-water training. Not the least of these reasons was that when I talked about my goal of swimming the English Channel, the members didn't look at me as if I were crazy. They'd been there, done that, even though it was a path less-traveled.

Getting ready for the Channel meant getting focused to the point of obsession. Everything I did, everything I thought, it seemed, led in one direction: from Dover to Calais. I sought out any and all information about this revered strip of water. This was before Google and laptops! I learned there had been nearly six thousand solo attempts at the crossing. Only two hundred and ninety-nine had been successful. Climbing Mount Everest had a better chance of success!

TRAINING SWIMS

My training swims took on a life of their own. I loved them, and I loved my swimming family. I knew I could count on them to be right alongside me, in kayaks and in the Zodiac boat, to fend off approaching ships and sail boats. I longed to venture outside the Aquatic Park cove. This required much planning, preparation, and approval by the club Swim Commissioner, Dave Zovickian, and I was thankful for his knowledge and dedication.

One of my eeriest swims took place when I left the Aquatic Park and swam around Alcatraz Island and back to the Dolphin Club. I saw the jail cells from a perspective available only from the icy waters of the Bay and for weeks afterward; I was haunted by the image of endless rows of bars. I knew that behind those bars were rooms no bigger than nine by eleven feet. "How ironic," I thought; that escape from any one of those cells would require prisoners to navigate the same water that was preparing me for the swim of my lifetime. I thought about the freedom the Bay symbolized to me, how freedom for one person can be prison for another.

Another challenging training swim I did was navigating a stretch of water the length of the Bay Bridge, from Berkley to San Francisco, and then down to the Golden Gate Bridge, totaling thirteen miles. As I approached Treasure Island, the current was starting to switch and I had to make it past the tip of the Island without running aground. Once I cleared it, I shot past and under the Bay Bridge, riding the current to the Golden Gate. I almost felt I was surfing; there is no fighting the powerful current in middle of the Bay.

Yet another favorite training swim occurred on New Year's Day 1992, when long-time arch-rivals, the Dolphin Club and South End Rowing Club, come together to do the "Escape from Alcatraz Polar Bear Swim." The evening before, I'd celebrated a New York New Year's party at my apartment with fellow Polar Bears. At nine o'clock the party ended, as we hibernated for the next few hours, in order to be fresh for our early morning swim.

We loaded onto the ferry at Fisherman's Wharf, and it shuttled us out to Alcatraz Island. We were not allowed to set foot on the Government-protected Island, and when I jumped off the edge of the ferry, I left the pack of swimmers and took the most direct route to Aquatic Park. During my open-water training, I had taught myself to do a front stroke: instead of turning my head to the right, I lifted my head and shoulders up out of the water, took a breath, and located my path homeward.

New Year's Day 1992 - Escape from Alcatraz Polar Bear Swim

When I finally reached the shore at the Dolphin Club, I was greeted by a camera crew asking questions about my swim, and seemingly amazed that anyone in their right mind would intentionally enter those waters at any time, much less on January 1st! I tried to talk but it wasn't easy; my jaw shook from near hypothermia, a result of swimming in 48°F water for thirty-six minutes. At first I wasn't sure why they were there and why they were interviewing me, but then I realized that I was the first woman ashore. Here I was, live on CNN, with "titty hard-on's"!

REINVENTING MYSELF AS KATE

The first step in my transformation from Kathryn to Kate, even before I joined the Dolphin Club, was to say goodbye to dutiful Kathryn and to welcome the adventurous Kate with open arms. Step two, joining the Dolphin Club, affected far more than my swimming. I discovered that my inner psyche was remolding itself. I was learning not only who I was but who I *wanted to be*. The Kate I welcomed would accept herself, not in spite of a buoyant personality but *because* of it! In fact, the Kate I welcomed was prepared to fully accept herself, with respect and joy.

Along with my psychic transformation, came another intriguing change. I never got sick. Not a cold. Not the flu. Not even a sniffle. To this day, I am convinced that cold-water swimming flushes the blood system and is detoxifying. The fact is, as long as I was training in the Bay, every day was exhilarating. I remember walking to work after a particularly strenuous morning swim, saying to myself, "World Come Get Me!" I was still high on endorphins, my whole body warm and drunk with happiness.

FULL MOON SWIM

My new-found office skills that I learned while working at Beringer Vineyards helped me land a job, working short-term for a fellow Dolphin member, during my cold-water training. My office, conveniently located in the Marina district was walking distance to the Dolphin Club. After work I often returned to my home-away-from-home, to meet other members for an evening swim. Dusk is a beautiful time at Aquatic Park, with the lights of the Ghirardelli Square sign casting their imposing and colorful reflection on the water. The only thing better than an evening swim at Aquatic Park, was swimming under a full moon. My friends agreed, and decided to try it with me. Soon there was a group of us gathering under the full moon, like werewolves in a pack. We swam out to the opening of Hyde Street pier. I started a tradition of saluting the Golden Gate Bridge by sticking a leg out of the water with the knee bent, then straightening it.

A couple of months after I started the Full Moon Swim, I came up with the idea of a "Full-Moon, Full Moon Swim". As soon as we got into the water, we whipped off our swim suits and threw them to shore. I found it nothing less than liberating to swim naked in the Bay. It also provided great entertainment for the tourists standing at the end of the Hyde Street pier!

As I approached my goal, I knew that I was about to write another chapter in my life. I was encouraged to go forth with my head above water, by my cherished Dolphin family, and knew I would look back on the last sixteen months in San Francisco as the best of times.

A DOLPHIN FOR LIFE!

Although I no longer live in the Bay area, I continue my out-of-town membership to the Dolphin Club. I receive e-mails on a daily basis from their Yahoo group and love keeping in contact vicariously through cyberspace. I left my heart in San Francisco! My dream is to return someday to Napa Valley and commute to the city for endorphins and "Phins".

What gives you an endorphin rush? Do you pursue that activity on a regular basis?

Have you ever committed to the serious pursuit of a goal? If so, did your focus on that goal lead to adventures you might never have otherwise experienced?

"Some goals are so worthy, it's glorious even to fail."
—Unknown

My English Channel Swim 6

Over to Dover

In mid-July of 1992, four days before I was scheduled to hop the pond, my brother Huck decided to go with me. He was welcome company for me and helped transport my luggage and swim paraphernalia, including: sleeping bag, gallon thermos, towels, power bars, electrolytes, and of course swim suits. I knew Huck, a triathlete, could and would swim with me at Dover. The youngest two of six children, he and I were very close and remain so today. It meant everything to me that he would be there to experience my goal with me.

My Captain

Huck and I settled into wonderful accommodations in the basement apartment of a bed and breakfast, and recovered from our jet-lag. The second day, we ventured out to meet the captain I had hired to escort me across the English Channel. He told me that I would be on standby for the swim. If the right conditions were forecast, he'd give me my 24-hour notice. I explained to him that my mother and stepfather were scheduled to arrive in two weeks to be on the boat with me. He said I needed to listen to him; he was responsible for getting me across the Channel.

Judgment Call

I knew it would break my mom's heart to not be there for my swim. She and Jack had supported my qualifying ten-hour swim in 60°F water, at Lake Sonoma in May, when we'd rented a "party barge" and they had skippered the boat alongside me for the trial swim. I'd had a ball with my endurance swim, actually picking up my pace to a near-sprint during the tenth hour. Not only did my parents run the boat, they also fed my crew of Dolphin Club friends. I owed them this opportunity to be with me for the Channel swim. They were my biggest supporters, and I wanted them there for both of our sakes. I called my mom and told her what the captain had said. With luck, the weather would cooperate with our original plan.

Suzanne from Australia

Huck and I went for our first swim at the smooth pebbled beach at Dover. Several groups of people were there preparing for their own swims as well. I met two girls from Australia. One of them, Suzanne, told me about the wild adventures that had accompanied her training. She swam off the northern Queensland shore in a shark-proof cage, which banged her around like a piece of popcorn in a kettle. She also told me of her harrowing experience swimming in Glacier Bay, Alaska, during cold-water training when, against her will; she was scooped up by the Coast Guard who tried to check her into a mental hospital. They thought she was trying to kill herself; I knew immediately we were kindred spirits!

JANICA FROM INDIA

Janica was a paraplegic as a result of childhood Polio. It was impossible to maneuver a wheelchair on the pebbled beach and she was trying to get to the water to swim. Huck picked her up and carried her into the water and, once in the surf, she swam like a fish, using her upper body strength. Huck helped her back into the wheelchair after her workout, and sitting down with her, we were astonished to hear that she, too, was aspiring to swim the Channel.

We later learned that her parents had brought her there to swim the English Channel in order to be recognized as a National Hero in India. If she succeeded in achieving that honor, her government would provide for her and her family. My heart went out to her.

THE KENNEDY CLAN

Farther down the shore, we saw a large group of people huddled together on the beach around one man, Michael Kennedy. If he had a successful swim, he would be the first man from Ireland to swim the English Channel. So many friends, family and media were there to support him; it already seemed like a celebration for all. Huck and I introduced ourselves and were immediately brought into their circle of friends. Mic, I could tell right away, was a character, a crass salty dog. He gave my brother Huck and me big hugs, as if we were long-lost relatives. Mic was Michael's right-hand man and coach, organizing all the details for his swim.

Several days later, Michael did swim the English Channel, successfully. The entire crossing was broadcast over the radio to the Dublin pubs, so the country could cheer him on. I was so happy for him, and his country, and was honored to have met him and his crew. The next day, there was a celebration on the Dover beach like no other. Mic asked me if he could board the boat for my swim. It brought tears to my eyes that he asked to be there, and of course I accepted his support.

MY 24-HOUR NOTICE

That afternoon, I got a call from Mike, my captain, giving me my 24-hour notice. I had to call my mom and tell her the news. At that point, I'd spent two intense years in training, and anticipation of the swim; I was a nervous wreck, and I just wanted to get it done and go on with my life. I needed to listen to Mike; he would get me across. The countdown began.

Two thumbs up on Dover's Shakespeare Beach, for my big swim on July 25, 1992. Photo courtesy of Mike Griggs, UK

Red Sky at Morn

Mic picked Huck and me up from our apartment at 4:15 a.m. I'd eaten my last warm bowl of oatmeal, hoping it would stick to my ribs for the swim. We approached the boat at the Dover wharf, where Mike Griggs, a professional photographer, waited to take my picture at that early dawn hour. He then drove to Shakespeare Beach to capture my start. There was a beautiful red sunrise over my shoulder.

I jumped off the boat, swam to shore and waited for my official start by the Channel Swim Association recorder on board. By the time I started my swim at 5:06 a.m., the sun was up and the water had a small chop. The whistle blew and excitedly, I began to swim.

There's France!

Five hours and twelve minutes later, I was half-way to France. The water was like glass and I knew I could make it. France looked so close; I fantasized about reaching shore and having a glass of champagne.

Forty-five minutes later, the storm broke and gale-force winds were upon me. I couldn't believe what was happening. Surely the pilot had known there was a storm forecast? Too busy preparing for my swim and writing all my excitement in my journal, I hadn't watched the evening news the night before.

I stopped to drink my electrolytes. At that moment a wave crashed over my head and I found myself chugging luke-warm salty liquid. That was when the crew decided to stop feeding me my warm replenishing lifeline. They knew all too well that salt water can change your blood chemistry, to the point of killing you. The waves continued growing in size, up to eight feet high. I was trying to swim uphill against a ruthless and powerful current. My body began to shut down. I became disoriented and swam away from the boat. They pulled me out of the water after eight hours and forty-three minutes.

They carried me to the bench on board and wrapped me in towels. All I could say was "Wa-wa-wa-what ha-ha-happened?" Mike explained that it was too much for me to be out there under those conditions; I don't really remember much else.

The waves were so big the crew on board the boat, were getting sea-sick. After an exhausting three-hour boat ride in the terrifying storm, we arrived back at Dover. I tried to get up and walk off the boat, but needed assistance; my body was shot from hypothermia and my equilibrium had not yet returned.

Finally at the Bed and Breakfast; I started to thaw in the warmth of the bath-tub's waters. I sat there in the hot water with saltwater still draining out of my nose. "Oh my God, what had happened to my goal? Was it out of reach forever?" I wanted to try again, under better conditions. I knew I could make it! I found my way to bed and slept.

The next day I told Huck I planned to swim again. He gave me a big hug and told me I needed to watch the video he had taken of my swim. Since we had only the viewfinder of the camera to watch from, I sat on his lap and watched the horrifying video. Even now, it brings tears to my eyes to recall this. I hadn't realized how close to death I had come. When they brought me on board the boat, and pulled off my goggles, my eyes were completely dilated. I had never seen anyone in such a state of hypothermia. Huck and I sat there and cried. My precious goal turned out to be something different from what I had thought. I gave the Channel crossing my best shot, but it was up to the Man Upstairs to determine the outcome. It would be some time before I properly appreciated what I had actually achieved.

Was it possible for me to be self-accepting even though I hadn't achieved the goal I'd envisioned? I'd given two years of my life to train for this one event. I'd moved to San Francisco and swum with the Dolphins. As I thought about the experiences of those two years, I realized that it wasn't reaching the goal that would define my success but the *path I had chosen to take to get there.*

Focusing so intensely on one goal taught me that I possessed qualities I had not been aware of. For example, I could be extremely determined. The only person I answered to was myself; if there was someone or something in my way, even if it was a job that I loved, with people I enjoyed, I was able to summon the determination to leave Beringer Vineyards, and move to San Francisco, where I needed to be to prepare for my shot at the Channel.

I learned that I could tolerate the blood, sweat, tears and time required to build endurance.

I had faith in myself. I knew I was physically and emotionally capable of swimming the English Channel. The actual distance is 21.45 miles, but currents alter the length of the swim anywhere from 35 to 50 miles. If I hadn't believed in myself, no amount of determination and endurance would have enabled me to succeed. I was prepared, and I never gave room in my psyche for self-doubt to creep in.

I discovered Kate! While I was in San Francisco, I discovered this wonderful, exuberant, adventurous person inside myself, far away from the Kathryn who was content, as Gail McCormick's husband, Bill, once told me, "clipping family coupons" in Portland, Oregon.

To this day, I have countless fond memories of that particular journey.

Have you ever experienced the company of kindred spirits, sharing the same passion, seeking to achieve similar goals?

It is not easy to accept falling short of a goal you have worked hard and long to reach. How do you manage to regroup when things do not work out as planned?

Kate Cronin Haslach

"It is one of the most beautiful compensations of life that no man can sincerely try to help another without helping himself."

—Ralph Waldo Emerson

English Channel Relays 7

JANICA'S RELAY

I resigned myself to the fact that my two-year journey was over. It was time to discover what would become of the rest of my life. My brother and I decided to rest up before making arrangements to fly back to the States. We thought it would be nice to do one last swim and catch up with our new friends at the beach.

Was it just a coincidence that when we got to the beach, we found a group of people organizing a relay? The captain of the boat Janica hired had concluded that she wasn't capable of swimming solo but that he would support her in a relay. My body was completely shot from my own solo attempt two days before, but nevertheless I wanted to take part in this relay; they weren't so sure about my brother, but Huck and I persuaded them that we *both* would pull our weight, plus some, on this relay...the very next day.

Since I was the fastest swimmer in the newly-formed group, I was chosen to start the first leg of the relay. It would also mean that I would most likely swim a third leg. I went out straight-away and bought groceries for the next day's journey.

The nice thing about swimming in a relay is that you only swim for one hour at a time, although it may still feel like the longest hour of your life. The relay arrangements gave my body five hours to recuperate on board the boat. Even though I was showing signs of hypothermia, my body involuntarily shaking after swimming all three legs, I was fortunate enough to regain my normal body temperature within an hour after getting back on the boat.

The relay was a big test for me to discover whether I had the strength and endurance to swim so soon after my solo attempt. Our relay team succeeded. We made it to the shore of Cap Gris-Nez in fourteen hours and forty-eight minutes. Huck and I were so thankful to get back to England the next morning at 4:30 a.m. We both agreed, next time we'd take a hovercraft to France!

There and then, my English Channel adventure was over. I'd learned so much about myself on the long journey to the Channel, and during the crossing itself; I was thankful for all the wonder-ful people I had met along the way. In particular, I would never forget the support of my fellow Dolphin Club members, who had put so much effort into encouraging me on my journey. I knew that some day I would make that same effort for someone else.

RETURNING TO PORTLAND

I got back from England exhausted. Jet-lag, or maybe the free drinks in business class, had taken their toll. Huck and I were mysteriously bumped up to business class. I almost turned the offer down because I didn't want to give up a window seat. Huck elbowed me, and we accepted.

I slept off my jet-lag over the next few days. I decided to not get out of bed until I felt almost human. After all, in the past ten days, I had attempted an English Channel solo swim and swum three legs of a relay. I deserved to be wiped out. Moreover, the pain on my mom's face was excruciating; she was so disappointed to have missed being there.

"Look on the bright side," I told myself. "There's a new chapter ahead." At the time I didn't know I would some day be an author.

THE FAMILY THING

When I returned from England I didn't know what was to become of me. I thought I'd give Portland one more try; as an adult this time. I started dating an old high-school friend while I figured out my career and living arrangements. Wanting independence, I moved into a great apartment in Northwest Portland that my mom's neighbor's son had recently vacated. The view overlooked the bridges and mountains surrounding Portland.

Since everybody in Portland had always known me as Kathryn, I once again assumed the name and being of the person I'd filed away two years before under "conventional". I effectively shut the door, both on Kate and on my dream of returning anytime soon to Napa Valley.

Fifteen months later I married my high-school friend, now my best friend, Tim Haslach. We soon started a family; eight and a half months later my precious daughter Caroline Leadbetter arrived. I had married a "man of height" and I needed a caesariansection in order to ensure the survival of mother and child. I was stunned to see such a long-limbed, pink, gorgeous baby come out of my body. I knew right away that she would be a great piano player, with those long fingers and indeed, she does have a gift for music, and has entertained me with her playing and singing.

Twenty-two months later, Caroline was joined by her baby brother Peter Thomas. Weighing nearly ten pounds, he was this cute roly-poly baby with dark hair. This time, I suggested the doctor simply put a zipper in me, when I gave birth by caesarian section for second time, since I clearly wasn't able to provide a normal exit. Peter, although not a piano player, has been tactile since birth. He has always explored the world by touching it with his fingers. I know someday he will make a living using his keen sense of touch, maybe as a sculptor.

I love being a mother. I wouldn't trade one second of it...well, maybe the two c-sections. I did not enjoy being eviscerated. Tim and I decided to stop there.

THE KAREN GAFFNEY RELAY

Nine years later and married with two wonderful children, opportunity knocked on my door. I was at my in-law's house for dinner and my father-in-law, Frank, handed me an article about a young girl with Downs Syndrome, living in Portland, who wanted someday to swim the English Channel. I immediately thought, "I bet I could put together a relay for her."

That very next week, I ran into Karen at the Multnomah Athletic Club's 50-meter pool, where I swim regularly. While talking with her, I told her of my adventures swimming the English Channel, and suggested she might, also, consider doing a relay. She told her parents about our conversation and invited me over to their house. I brought along the videos of both of my swims and strongly suggested it would be in Karen's best interest if we put together a relay. They agreed.

My first phone call was to Gail Bowen McCormick. A mentor and role model for me, Gail had made her own solo attempt many years earlier. Swimming for nearly twelve hours, she had less than two miles to go to shore when the current shifted and she spent the last hour swimming without making any progress towards shore, before being pulled onto the boat. She was the person who taught herself to speak backwards during her swim. She agreed right there and then to be a part of this relay.

The second call was to Joe Tennant. We'd swum "Across the Columbia River" on Labor Day weekend together when he told me that someday he wanted to swim the English Channel. He also suggested that we talk with his brother Mike, who lived in Bend and was a big open-water swimmer.

Since I'd married a competitive swimmer, I also included my husband Tim in the plan for this relay. In fact, so many people wanted to take part in this historic event, the first person with Downs Syndrome to swim the English Channel, that we formed two separate relays.

I have to say Gail was our champion. We were all excited about the event, but it was Gail whose unbridled enthusiasm inspired us all. She organized *big* fundraisers for our relay teams, and involved the media. I soon found myself being interviewed by the local broadcasters. I was so honored to help Karen Gaffney live her dream of swimming the English Channel.

Team Gaffney Members, front row: Sarah Quan, Kelsey Bowen, Kate Haslach, Lindy Mount, Karen Gaffney, Gail McCormick, and Laura Schob. Back row: Camillo Bruce, Brian Gaffney, Tom Landis, Tim Haslach, Joe Tennant, Mike Tennant, and Marc Bowen.

The day the Karen Gaffney Relays took place, July 23, 2001, it was actually hot in southern England! The weather couldn't have been better; the water was calm the whole way. It proved to me that I had gone full circle in my adventure; everything had turned out the way it was supposed to have been. It was astonishing how many coincidences there had been: our showing up at the beach the day they were organizing Janica's relay, my running into Karen the very next week after reading about her, not to mention having such an amazing group of people form to help Karen live her dream. I was learning that my journey toward self-acceptance was to be a life-long adventure, full of surprises!

When opportunity knocks on your door, do you answer it?

Team Gaffney was created by combining many individual minds, experiences and energies; it became a force bigger than ourselves, and its success belonged to all team members. Have you ever experienced the power of a group focused on a single goal, large or small?

"Well done is better than well said."

—Ben Franklin

The Gulping Gourmet 8

START A COOKING CLUB

As you already know, the overriding purpose of this book is to help other women become more self-accepting. One way to do this is to start a group of some kind. For me, it's always been cooking clubs. Wherever I lived as an adult, I started one. My first Gulping Gourmet emerged in Portland in the mid-eighties. Later when I lived in Calistoga, the Napa Valley Culinary Alliance filled my need for camaraderie, so it wasn't until I moved to San Francisco that another Gulping Gourmet was born. That one was especially wonderful because it gave me opportunities to make new friends and see parts of the city and gorgeous residences that I would never otherwise have experienced. Our dinners were not limited to geographical boundaries. We dined in the wine country, tailgated at Candlestick Stadium, and partied in the parks. After returning to Portland and starting a family, I organized four more Gulping Gourmets right in my neighbor-hood. I remain a member of Gulping Gourmet II to this day.

It's Easy and Fun to Start

The first thing I did was make a list of people I knew in my neighborhood and ask them if they knew anyone who might like to join our group. Once people heard I was starting a cooking club, my phone rang off the hook and each membership slot was quickly filled. After forming my first group of fourteen women, I realized I needed to start a waiting list to form the next group. That's how I happened to organize Gulping Gourmets II, III and IV in my neighborhood. The good news is that when you orga-nize your own group, you are the one determining the number of members and whether it's for singles, couples, women only, or whatever you please. For my groups, fourteen is the magic number for starters.

The unique thing about my cooking clubs is that they are de-signed to be fun and easy for everyone. While the host chooses the dinner theme, she doesn't do any of the cooking. Organizing the house is enough of a challenge. The only thing she needs to pre-pare is coffee service after dinner. Everyone else brings the food. I've seen other groups where the host prepares the whole dinner for everyone. That is way too much work. Assigning one dish per person ensures that everyone shares the responsibilities. Another advantage is that once the rotating schedule is set up, everyone knows what to bring, from month to month. The guests bring wine, cocktails, appetizer, salad, vegetable, entrée, or dessert, in that order. For example, if you bring the salad in July, you'll be bringing the vegetable in August and the entrée in September.

GUIDELINES

Although you will certainly infuse your group with your own personality and shape it to your own needs, it's always helpful to have some guidelines when starting something new. Following is a "snapshot" of a typical Gulping Gourmet session. Your picture may look quite different, but this should provide a good idea of what you might see.

Typically, we arrive at the host's house at 6:30 p.m. for cocktails and appetizers, and at 7:30 p.m. we are seated for dinner. People bringing cocktails and appetizers typically drop their items off early if they know they are not going to be there right on time. If we need to put our food in the oven at the host's house, we call her ahead of time so she can preheat the oven and coordinate it with any other foods needing to be baked or heated. Each person is responsible for having her dish ready to serve by 7:30 p.m.

We also have a regrets only policy. If the host doesn't hear from members one week in advance, she assumes her guests will be attending the dinner.

CREATIVE THEMES

Each month it's up to the hostess to be as creative as she wants for the dinner at her house. Of course, it's always wise to alert your group as far in advance as possible what your theme is, and best if you do it at the prior dinner. That way, everyone will have time to research recipes...and costumes! E-mail reminders are always helpful.

Traditional Themes

Cooking with citrus, foods that start with the letter "P" (or any other letter of the alphabet), low-fat foods, these are just a few of the unusual themes that people have come up with in the past. Then there are the ethnic food choices such as Thai, French, Italian, Caribbean, etc; the possibilities are endless. Another popular idea is to choose a specific month's issue of a food magazine and have everyone try a new recipe. We had a Martha Stewart dinner and I brought a carrot cake with a file stuck in the middle of the cake. (Martha was in jail at the time.)

Then there are the holiday events, like Valentine's Day, St. Patrick's Day, Cinco de Mayo, Fourth of July, and Oktoberfest, all of which can be used as a monthly theme. One Valentine's Day we prepared aphrodisiacs for our meal. The husbands couldn't wait for us to get home!

Wedding Reception

I loved the wedding reception dinner theme. It gave everyone a chance to dust off their outdated once-worn, bridesmaid's dresses, whether or not they still fit. I had to use safety pins to close the back of my bridesmaid's dress. We all had so much fun talking about the wedding parties we attended and laughing at each other's outdated gowns as we sipped on champagne and hors d'oeuvres. If anyone dares, they can come as the bride.

Pajama Party

One month we all wore pajamas and pigtails and ate popcorn, pizza and red licorice for dinner. Only this time, as adults, we also included alcohol. It made for plenty of giggles and rambunctious behavior.

Tailgater
While I was living in San Francisco, our group met at a Giants game. I think we spent most of the time at our cars eating and drinking, instead of watching baseball. I can't even tell you who the Giants played that evening. I'm not a huge baseball fan, but boy, did I have fun at that game!

Another nice thing about a tailgater, which can be done at home, is that paper plates and plastic utensils and plastic cups are totally acceptable to serve the food and drink.

Take-Out
One month a host chose take-out food for our theme. We brought boxes of pizza, Chinese and Thai food. The desserts came from local bakeries, and all the food was outstanding.

HOLIDAY PARTY
Every other year during the holidays, we have our dinner party and actually invite our husbands. We exchange white elephant gifts with each other. One time my husband and I received furry hand-cuffs! We also played a game which involved the husbands getting up in front of everyone and saying something about their wife that nobody else knew. Warning! This can be very dangerous!

Then on the alternate year, it's women only meeting for lunch at a special restaurant in town. Afterwards, we shop 'til we drop. Whoever the December host is decides for the group where we will be going, and makes the reservations.

A NIGHT OUT ON THE TOWN

August tends to be a traveling time for many of our members, so we know in advance that our group will be small this month. Turning lemons into the proverbial lemonade, we use this as an opportunity to dine at a lovely restaurant and enjoy special conversation with one another. This is a case where small is definitely beautiful.

COMPILE RECIPES

Getting everyone else's recipes will be another benefit you'll receive from your Gulping Gourmet Club. Today it's easy to compile and share all the great menus and recipes you experience at your cooking club get-togethers. Simply ask each person to send an e-mail with the recipe to the hostess of a particular session; she in turn will compile them and send them on to you, the Gulping Gourmet Chief! In my groups, we collect recipes monthly and at the end of the year distribute them all to our members. Everyone loves this process because we've all tasted the recipes and know in advance which ones we want to literally take home to our own kitchens.

DINNER AT MY HOUSE

I look forward to our Gulping Gourmet dinner each month and I especially look forward to having it at my home. In addition to anticipating the camaraderie which accompanies each of our sessions, I get to take out my crystal glasses, my best silverware, and my fine china! It took me far too many years to realize that organizing my table in preparation for a lovely meal can be a creative and artistic process. A memorable meal is definitely more than the food, alone.

When the evening arrives, my husband Tim takes our children, Caroline and Pete, out to dinner and I enjoy a hot bubble-bath before my guests arrive. It's a great tradition that I honor before any entertaining, requiring only a little organization on my part.

As we get older and become empty-nesters, we will need friends and important relationships more than ever. The Gulping Gourmet Clubs have been fabulous vehicles to bring those things into my own life. I encourage you to try your own version of the Gulping Gourmet Club. I am confident you will treasure the results.

If you'd like help starting your own Gulping Gourmet Club, just visit my website, www.KateHaslach.com, where you'll find all the forms and suggestions you'll need to make the experience a grand success for everyone involved.

Do you ever wish you had a bigger network of good friends? A club that meets monthly is a great way to widen your social circle in a positive way.

If you don't already belong to one, what kind of club might you be interested in starting or joining? Make it something you really enjoy doing! For example, besides the cooking itself, I love dreaming up themes for my cooking clubs, and then figuring out how to make them work. One of these days I'm going to throw a "Titanic" party, get everyone dressed in period clothing and set all the furniture aslant!

What sparks your creativity? What skills or interests would you thoroughly enjoy sharing with others?

Kate Cronin Haslach

"Think big thoughts, but relish small pleasures."

—H. Jackson Brown, Jr.

Wine Country Experiences 9

MY 40TH BIRTHDAY PRESENT

My mother is the most amazing person I've ever met. How in God's name did she survive raising six children, let alone giving birth to all of us? I think her best quality is that she has always been fair to all of her children. Even while enduring congestive heart-failure, she let each of us choose a destination, anywhere in the world, for us to celebrate our 40th birthday with her. Luckily, we weren't all born in the same year!

SONOMA MISSION INN

My mother and I both share a passion for gardening and cooking, and I couldn't wait to return to Napa Valley. So, in May of 2001, for my 40th birthday present, it was no surprise to anyone that I chose to revisit the Wine Country. We started off at the Sonoma Mission Inn, where we ate delicious spa food and enjoyed decadent treatments for two full days. That was my first over-night exposure to the wonderful world of exquisite dining and pampering.

Walking around the lush grounds, I saw two people in the hot-pool, one floating on her back on the surface of the water, while the other, a water therapist, gently embraced her. I asked one of the employees what they were doing and she explained that the therapist was giving a Watsu® Massage treatment, which is a relaxing body treatment in 96°F water, combining shiatsu massage, stretching, and energy work. I had never seen this ther-apy before and I thought it would be very nurturing.

Later that afternoon, before my paraffin wax dip manicure and pedicure, I noticed that the hot-pool was vacant. I put on my swim suit and got into the most wonderful water tempera-ture I had ever experienced. Unlike the water of many hot-tubs, it wasn't too hot or turbulent. I simply relaxed in the water and visualized a Watsu® massage. As I closed my eyes and drifted, I realized I was floating gently on the surface of the water, without any assistance. I could hear the soothing sound of the jets circu-lating the hot water in this wet Garden of Eden. My body went completely limp and my buoyancy crept up on me and caressed me into a deep meditative state. It was like nothing I had ever experienced in my world of water.

I'm not sure how long I was in the pool, but when at last I got out, I knew I had just experienced something magical. I took a cleansing shower and moisturized my body before my hand and foot treatments. I slept like a lumberjack that night and probably sounded like one too.

WINE COUNTRY INN

The next morning my mother and I checked out of the hotel and drove into Napa Valley over the road known locally as The Grapevine. It was a gorgeous late spring day. The smell of mustard blossoms gave me a flashback of my two years spent in St. Helena, working for Beringer Vineyards and of my adorable cottage in Calistoga. I was excited at the prospect of seeing Hugh Carpenter again and attending his Camp Napa Culinary.

Years earlier when I was living in Santa Monica, I actually worked with Hugh, sort of. I had a great job getting all the preparation done for his cooking classes at the well-known Montana Mercantile. I remember measuring out all the ingredients and put them into small glass ramekins, and there was Hugh, demonstrating the procedure for making Peking Duck. The class was spellbound and I, too, was saucer-eyed when he took a bicycle-tire pump with a basketball needle attached, pierced the duck's shoulder, and blew the skin up like a balloon. It was totally disgusting to me to see the poor duck, head and all, undergoing this procedure. Yes, the duck was dead!

Next stop on my birthday-present tour had mother and me checking into the Wine Country Inn for the duration of the renowned five-day cuisine and garden program. We quickly discovered a shared camaraderie with the other participants from all over North America, as we sat on the stone deck in the back yard, enjoying the iridescent sunset as we sampled some of Napa Valley's finest wine.

A NEW WATER EXPERIENCE

Bright and early the next morning, I realized that I would need plenty of exercise during my stay to make up for my increased intake of calories from sampling the cooking-class recipes. Turning naturally to water, I jumped into the Inn's palm tree-lined pool and swam short laps, not bothering to count, just enjoying the sensation of an increased heart rate.

After an exhilarating swim, I thought I'd see if I could float in this luke-warm oasis as I had in the hot pool at Sonoma Mission Inn. In the back of my mind, I guess I still thought that maybe the hot water at the Sonoma Mission Inn might have had something to do with my buoyancy, that perhaps the water itself was special. I soon learned that it wasn't. For a second glorious time, I found myself floating, just like a marshmallow in a cup of hot chocolate.

This time, I tried stretching while afloat in the water, to lengthen my aquatic muscles. I then played with the idea of doing aerobic exercises and stretches simultaneously, water snow angels, of a sort. This was something else new in my gilled aquatic experience. Then I tried floating on my back in the water, I reached for my ankles by bending my knees and arching my spine. It was quite challenging for me to keep my lungs filled with air for buoyancy and to stay relaxed at the same time. What was I doing?!

Then it struck me…Fat Chicks Float Well! I decided right there and then to share this experience with other people of buoyancy, both physical and psychic. That evening on the deck, during a happy hour of wine tasting and Napa Valley tidbits, I described my idea to my fellow guests. They gave me funny looks and said

"What?" I told them I was going to write a book called *Fat Chicks Float Well*. My mom pretended not to know me, and the ladies giggled and said they wanted the first copy of my book.

If you were to take a vacation with your mother, your sister, your cousin, your daughter or a close female friend, where would you choose to go with that particular companion, and why?

If you have never tried one, and you think a spa vacation might be something you would enjoy, why not go for it?

My life-long love of the water led me to discover the gift of buoyancy that has sustained me far beyond the experience of floating in the hot pool at the Sonoma Mission Inn. Are you doing something you feel passionate about? Has it led you to discover your own special gift?

"Relax; goodness will rise to the top."

—Kate Cronin Haslach

Buoy, Can I Float

I can't remember a time in my life when I couldn't float. When I was a child, I might not have admitted to my buoyancy, or even noticed it. However, now that I have an abundance of it, I've learned to enjoy the phenomenon and actually take advantage of it. I never claimed to be a *Sports Illustrated* swimsuit model and I don't let my abundant appearance in a swimsuit stop me from exercising in the water. People often stop me and ask if I am still swimming and I reply "Yes, and I float really well these days too!"

I've heard that swimmers are among the few athletes who actually develop fat within their muscle tissue or, as the beef industry calls it, "marbling." I guess that means I'm well-marbled. The fact is, all this marbling has helped me keep afloat and I'm not complaining. I'd love to test this theory and see if Michael Phelps, eight-time Olympic gold medalist swimmer, can float.

Before I flew to Dover in 1992, I knew that I was at my peak as far as physical fitness was concerned. I had myself tested to see what my lean body-mass was. At the time, I weighed 138 pounds and my body fat was just 12 percent. That meant that my lean body-mass was at 88 percent, and I still floated. Wow! If I'd been at my present weight when I swam the English Channel, I could have put up a sail and bobbed across!

In all my time in the water, the only people I've seen who were absolutely unable to float were on the Oregon State Wrestling Team. We shared the pool with the wrestlers after our morning weight-training workout and I could see all those poor lean body-mass anchors clinging on to the side of the pool for their dear lives. Of course, it would have helped if they had known how to swim.

The nice thing about buoyancy is that you don't need a huge body of water to experience the sensation. I steal every opportunity. For example, the first thing I do when getting into a hot-tub is roll over on my back and float away. All this floating means, of course, that my hair is almost constantly immersed in chlorinated water. I've spent a fortune on shampoo and conditioner, but it's all worth it.

LISTEN TO THE SOUND OF WATER

While I'm floating in a hot-tub, I close my eyes and listen to the sounds the water makes with the jets off, it's beautifully soothing. I feel myself transported back to the quiet and safety of the womb.

Floating—or at least *great* floating—requires that you be relaxed. If I'm rigid and fighting against my own buoyancy, my weight won't be evenly distributed. I imagine my thighs and upper arms helping me, as if I had water wings on.

Water Safety Instruction at the University of Arizona

At the University of Arizona, I took a water-safety class and, after getting certified, took a summer job as a lifeguard. In Oregon, thirteen months earlier, Mount St. Helens had violently erupted, filling the air with clouds of black ash and caused a dark, grimy, overcast summer throughout the entire fallout area, including Portland. In other words, not fun. So my new job in Arizona meant more to me than just a way to earn some much-needed money. I now had an excuse not to be in Portland that summer.

Lungs as Life Preservers

In my water-safety class I'd learned to use the air in my lungs to aid my floating. Simply by filling my lungs with air and holding my breath, I could immediately increase my buoyancy. I learned to take a slow, exaggerated inhale and hold it. Then I'd take a quick exhale and once again return to a slow inhale and hold. I'd repeat this process again. And again. And again.

Feet Down, Fingertips Up

Even though I knew I could float as is, I also learned a procedure to evenly distribute my body weight in the water. This was achieved by floating with my arms out straight from their sockets, palms up, and slowly bending my knees to a 90° angle until my ankles were directly below my knees. At the same time I would slowly raise my arms, as if doing a snow angel in the water. With my arms raised above my head, I bent my wrists to bring my fingertips out of the water. Now, all I had to do was relax and enjoy my buoyancy. Wherever I floated, eyes closed, I listened to the sounds of the water and was as relaxed as I've ever been. If I found myself floating under the moonlight, I would open my eyes and pretend I was floating in space.

WATER YOGA

Water and Yoga go together like salt and pepper. It was when I put the two together that I truly discovered how my special gift of buoyancy allows me to appreciate my body just the way it is. I've found that the combination of water and yoga is especially effective after a long-distance swim. I remember how much fun I had at the Wine Country Inn experiencing my buoyancy in every yoga position imaginable. Sometimes I think I must look like an otter floating on my back effortlessly, all the while stretching my muscles and putting my mind into a glorious state of meditation.

The meditation technique I use is one I made up a long time ago. I call it Trinity Breathing. Methodically and slowly I inhale to the count of five. Counting to five again, I hold my breath, and then exhale slowly and carefully to the count of five. It's three sets of counting to five, inhale, hold, and exhale. I do this until I am mentally in another place. All of a sudden, my mind moves away from issues and problems and toward living in the now; the sensation is almost an out-of-body experience. In addition to putting my mind in another place, water-yoga allows me to relax and move my arms and legs into positions I find difficult to do standing. For example, I can easily assume the tree posture lying on the surface of the water without worrying about keeping my balance or getting my foot to rest above the knee on the opposite leg. I also like to challenge myself by moving into the jellyfish position, one that I made up. Lying on my back, I drop my arms, arch my back and grab my ankles. I need to fill my lungs with as much air as possible in order to stay afloat.

And then there's my version of the downward dog, where I grab the pool's gutter and lean back with my rump against the side of the pool. With my legs resting in a V-shape against the wall of the pool, and toes out of the water, I can use my buoyancy to ease my legs apart to whatever distance comes naturally. It might look a little silly to passers-by, but being able to stretch under water is well worth any ridicule.

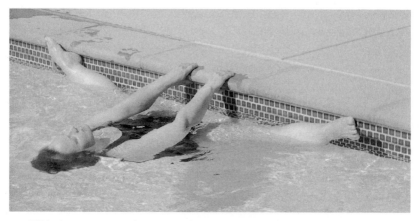

This is a picture of me stretching in the pool at Solage Calistoga during spring break 2009.

ADJUSTING TO GRAVITY

When I've had enough of water and yoga, I head straight for a cleansing shower. Then for the real frosting on the cake, I relax in the sunroom. Even though the sunroom's temperature is about 160°F, its dry heat can be tolerated longer than a sauna without sapping my energy. Despite its name, don't expect to get tanned. There, doing my Trinity Breathing once again, I give my body a few minutes to reacquaint itself with gravity.

HYDRATION

As you can imagine, with all the water contact I have, I'm soaked regularly in chlorine.

This means that I have to be very careful to use plenty of moisturizer all over my body to keep my skin from shriveling up like a dried prune. My solution? Slather, slather, slather. You're right. I don't buy just one bottle of moisturizer at a time.

In addition to a healthy slathering of my outside, I drink water obsessively after every swim to hydrate my body from the inside out. When I have time, I treat myself to a cinnamon spiced tea with a lemon wedge and read a section of the newspaper in the women's lounge before I return to reality. Then I'm off and running: more accurately put, I'm chasing children or horses.

Even if you think you are not a water person, would you be willing to try some of the things I have described in this chapter, such as floating in a pool and practicing Trinity Breathing?

If being in water makes you too uncomfortable to relax and focus, would you participate in other activities that involve conscious use of the breath, or meditation, such as yoga, or a martial art?

"That it will never come again,
Is what makes life so sweet."

—Emily Dickinson

Chunky Dunky 11

If you haven't started your own "Bucket List," believe me, you're never too young (or too old) to get your priorities in order. And way at the top of that "Do-Before-I-Die" list must be old-fashioned skinny-dipping, or what I affectionately term Chunky Dunky. Now, let me be clear: skinny-dipping is not about displaying your body to the world, nor is it about putting yourself in danger; best of all is that being skinny isn't a requirement. My hunch is that you'll find—as I did—that the simple act of skinny-dipping will be your ultimate "baptism of self-acceptance."

Skinny-dipping is very versatile. You can do it by yourself or with your birds-of-a-feather-float-together friends. You can do it in the dark or in broad daylight in the privacy of someone's back yard, preferably a someone you know! Personally, my favorite location for a Full-Moon, Full Moon splash is off the dock of the Dolphin Club, along the Aquatic Park in San Francisco. I love the Ghirardelli billboard lights reflecting off the Bay water, the sounds of the city bustling around me, the endorphin rush of the cold water penetrating my body, the beam of moonlight guiding my soul towards self-acceptance. It is a life-affirming experience. There, of course, I also have the advantage of jumping into a hot shower and sauna immediately afterwards at the Dolphin Club. If you're really not into cold-water submersion, a great alternative is a hot-tub which allows you to take the plunge any time of year.

GULPING GOURMET DIP
The subject of skinny-dipping is never far away when I'm thinking about self-acceptance and self-discovery, which means it can pop up just about anytime, and anyplace! I especially remember its coming up one hot September evening at my friend Jennifer's house during a meeting of our neighborhood cooking group, Gulping Gourmet II. We were seated around the outdoor wood deck near the pool, enjoying our cocktails, as the sky turned a luscious-looking Moroccan orange.

During dinner I started to tell other members about this book and my own journey toward self-acceptance. You won't be surprised that I emphasized the positive effects of skinny-dipping and what a difference it could make in their own struggle to accept themselves. As if on cue, one of my friends suggested I go skinny-dipping in Jennifer's pool right then and there. "Ok," I said, and invited them all join me for a little moonlit splash. My friends just sat there and giggled at the idea. The giggles got louder as I quickly stripped off all my clothes and jumped in the pool. Swimming back and forth, I honored my friends on the deck with a particularly elegant Golden Gate Salute.

Suddenly, a bright flash went off and I realized a picture had been taken. I promptly warned that I didn't plan to have my picture on the internet, so whoever the culprit was should push the camera's delete button. Continuing my float around the pool, I wished I had my own camera to capture the looks of amazement and, I thought, envy, on their faces.

Jennifer finally brought a beach towel out for me and I agreed that I'd had enough skinny-dipping for the evening. As I wrapped the towel around myself, I could see that the girls were still in shock that I had actually done this, as they continued to giggle. Our Gulping Gourmet II group has been meeting for ten years and although we all know each other pretty well, this was the first time Kate had attended. And they thought they knew Kathryn!

As we departed that evening, they all admitted what I had suspected: they wished that they, too, had joined me in taking the plunge. Maybe next time!

RESERVOIRATIONS

While I was living in Calistoga, I used to mountain-bike all over the valley with my boyfriend, Bart. There weren't any public pools that we could just jump into without paying some kind of fee, so when the summer heat reached blistering levels and perspiration ran off our bodies like hot rain, we did the sensible thing. We headed straight for the cool waters of the many vineyard reservoirs dotting the valley.

Perhaps you, too, have had the good fortune to travel through the Napa Valley, though probably not on a mountain bike. You'll remember that topping the many hills surrounding the Valley lie the gorgeous properties of well-known vintners. Mountain bikes have many advantages, not the least being that you can get off the beaten tourist path quickly, which is what we used to do. With our backpacks filled with "survival gear": fresh carrot juice; energy bars; a thermos of fresh drinking water, we were experts at finding the cooling waters otherwise intended for grapes! Since Bart and I had long since left modesty behind, we could strip down quickly and fully enjoy our free reservoiration swims.

There were a few downsides to these expeditions. I once got a heavy dose of poison oak packing my bulky bike up the unbeaten path while navigating a hillside. I also learned that the terrain we covered was shared by heat-loving rattlesnakes, and that there was some kind of black water-snake in the reservoirs. Luckily, my only contact with snakes was picking up rattles I found on the dusty pathway. On the bright side, we also found carved obsidian arrowheads from the many Native American tribes who had inhabited the valley centuries earlier.

Dating Bart was like being in an Indiana Jones movie, full of death-defying adventures. His father was a photographer for National Geographic and offered his two children a Chromacolor upbringing in Central America. When Bart and I ended our relationship I genuflected in thanks to the universe for my survival.

DIPPING INTO CHILDHOOD
Growing up in the Sixties gave me a unique perspective on skinny-dipping. Once during one of the many cocktail parties my parents hosted, Mother, Huck and I sneaked down to the family pool, hidden in the garden far below our house for, what else? A quick skinny- dip, of course! Since we needed to be quiet so our

guests wouldn't hear us splashing about, Mother taught us to do the Vietnam Stroke, which allowed us to swim quietly without making a ripple in the water. We mastered the silent swimming; it was the giggles we needed to contain!

THE LITTLE GIRL IN ME

Maybe it was competitive swimming, the locker-room upbringing that tore the modesty right off my back. Even during the awkward adolescent years, we joked about our rosebuds blooming. I think that sense of humor will help me through menopause, as I tuck my breasts into my belt.

If you have a "Bucket List" what are the things you'd like to do before you die?

Might skinny-dipping be one of those things? Skinny-dipping is not about exposing your body to the world. It is the gloriously sensual experience of water touching your bare skin as you swim, a powerful sense of physical and spiritual freedom.

Would you consider going skinny-dipping if no-one saw you doing it?

How comfortable are you in your own skin, naked or clothed, in or out of water?

Kate Cronin Haslach

"A friend is a person with whom I may be sincere. Before him, I may think aloud."

—Ralph Waldo Emerson

Relatively Blessed 12

Being an aqua nut, I tend to judge the depth of a person's character in terms of water. That said, my mother is my ocean. I have no idea how she coped with six children. I'm barely able to handle two.

When she was in her forties, Mother discovered that she had a heart condition that showed up as a heart murmur. She always insisted it originated in a bout with rheumatic fever she had as a young child. Eventually, she had her heart valves replaced and then a pace-maker implanted. Then we got the devastating news that she had congestive heart failure.

My Mother has always been the Rock of Gibraltar for us six children. She was as fit as an ox and walked like a nomadic tribal chief. It was hard to see her health decline so rapidly.

By the Grace of God

At seventy-one, Mother was going to have a heart transplant. Or-dinarily, people in their seventies aren't even eligible to be on the "A" rating waiting-list, but since she'd taken such amazing care of her health, an exception was made. She was now eligible to receive a heart of any age for her transplant.

Her waiting-list time was grueling for all of us. At one point, we all knew she had only days to live if something were not done. With no other choice available, Mother was admitted to the hospital. And, by the grace of God, after only six days, we got the call: a new heart was ready for her. I immediately hung up the phone and made reservations to fly down to Los Angeles. And, with God's further help, I got to see my mother for two minutes before she went into surgery. I knew this was a sign things were going to turn out well. And they did.

Mother survived the marathon surgery performed by a fabu-lous team of UCLA doctors and nurses. Not a day goes by that I'm not thankful for my mother's thirty-nine-year-old heart, and grateful to the woman who, in losing her own life, saved my Mother's. My way of showing my appreciation will be to make my own organs available to someone else when the time comes.

Sense of Humor

If it weren't for my mom's keen sense of humor, she would have never survived her ordeal. She has always made me laugh with her self-deprecating remarks. After checking out of UCLA hospi-tal, she threatened my step-dad Jack with a seventh child!

I'll never forget the story of my mom, her sister, my Aunt Sally, and Gammy shopping for girdles in the late 1960's. My grandmother tried on the new Playtex Living Girdle, which was built like a tire, and found herself unable to take it off. The three of them broke out into giggles. I can just see the three of them hunched over trying desperately to control their bladders in the dressing room, in fits of uncontrollable laughter, with tears running down their faces.

ELIZABETH ANN

I can hear my Aunt Sally say to my cousin Betsy, "Elizabeth Ann, you have been spending way too much time with Kathryn. You are beginning to talk fast like her." Betsy and I are just like our mothers. We are less than five months apart and have been best friends forever.

One Christmas, Betsy and I hid under the huge carved-wood Gothic dinning-room table. We were probably seven years old. We were stuck there listening to our parents boasting about what awful children the two of us were. They had absolutely no idea we were there, drinking in every word and swelling with pride.

SUN VALLEY BLAST

In our early twenties, Betsy and I vacationed together. One spring break, during college, we flew to Sun Valley, Idaho. It will never be the same! We had so much fun making idiots of ourselves, riding the chairlifts backwards, partying at Slavies Tavern; just being young and dumb. Those were the days.

On our return flight home we practically lost our voices reminiscing about our Sun Valley adventure. We got off the plane, still so caught up in our conversation that we walked in the opposite direction from the terminal. Finally, my mom and aunt caught

FAT CHICKS FLOAT WELL

up with us, whereupon Betsy and I went into an uncontrolled laughing fit. We both leaned over and waddled into the nearest restroom.

THE BIG GAME

Talk about young and dumb...I was to blame for this one. Betsy had just graduated from University of Oregon and I had transferred from the University of Arizona to Oregon State. I talked Betsy into driving to Corvallis for the U of A versus OSU football game. We went out to the local pizzeria, which was packed with college students anticipating the game. After a pitcher of beer and pizza, we drove to Reser Stadium only to find the lights out. That's when we figured out the game was in Tucson. Luckily, we weren't wearing girdles and no one saw us there at the stadium, hunched over in the grip of a giggle attack.

COMEDY NIGHT

I'll tell you just one more story. After college Betsy and I lived in Portland and decided to meet at the Leaky Roof Tavern for comedy night. During the break, I noticed that the microphone was still sitting up on stage connected to a long cord. When we got up to use the restroom, it was easy for me to quickly grab the mike and hide it behind my back without anyone noticing. Once we got into the bathroom, I began the interview, asking my cousin about her nonexistent sex life. She proceeded to make up a funny story of her fantasy love life. Poor Betsy: the sound of her peeing and the fantasy story was being broadcast to the entire bar. After she flushed the toilet and came out of the stall, she realized what I had done. Thank God she has a sense of humor. Anyone else would have killed me. When we got back to our table, the audience gave us a standing ovation.

Betsy and I lead busy lives and these days we need to plan weeks in advance to share time together. I cherish every second I spend with her.

I am perfectly happy with the idea of donating my organs after my death, but I don't want my body used as a classroom cadaver. Do you have reservations about donating your organs? Why, or why not?

I am blessed to have a cousin who is also such a great friend. Even when Betsy and I are far apart, I know we are only a heart-beat away. Do you feel this way about someone in your life?

I like the fact that Betsy understands and enjoys Kate. Maybe that is why we get along so well! Do you have a close friend who welcomes and encourages your playful side?

"The heart that loves is always young"
—Anonymous (Greek Proverb)

The Kate in Me

MY FIRST GIRDLE

In 1999, for my thirty-eighth birthday celebration, my husband and I bought a table to the interactive play *Tony & Tina's Wedding*. We invited five other couples to join us for the hilarious play and dinner-dance. All of us dressed up in loud, over-the-top wedding attire. Tim wore a maroon button-down shirt with an obnoxious tie. I wore my long, skinny black dress and my grandmother's ocelot fur coat.

To make me appear slimmer under the long black dress, I wore a girdle. Yes, a real girdle! I also soon found myself muttering a variety of colorful things, including, "How the heck am I supposed to sit down, let alone breathe, in one of these contraptions?" How in the world had my own mother and grandmother survived being scrunched like that for all those years?

MY LAST GIRDLE

Several years of jazz dance training during elementary and high school made it easy for me to feel I was really a part of the wedding party. So, when the father of the groom invited me to dance on top of the wedding party's table, I was there in the proverbial heartbeat. It also took no longer than that heartbeat for me to realize that I was in girdle prison and that dancing was going to be a near-impossibility with that contraption on. So I did the logical thing; I took it off. Shimmying it down to my ankles, I kicked it into the audience, hoping never to see it again. Captured in the moment, I felt a huge relief just getting the damn thing off. Besides, everyone was laughing!

AUDITIONS!

After the song ended, I got off the table without breaking my neck and went back to my table. As soon as I got there, two people from the backstage crew invited me into the hallway. I thought they wanted to make sure I wasn't too intoxicated or maybe they wanted to have me thrown in jail. I sat down with them and said I was just having fun and I'd only had two gin and tonics. They asked me if I wanted to audition for the play!

THE RADIO INTERVIEW

A couple years later, "Tony" and "Tina" were interviewed on the radio and asked what some of their most memorable moments were from all the years of performing their legendary play. They told the story about some girl who got on the wedding party's table and took her *underpants* off and threw them into the audience. No wonder everyone was laughing!

REAL BOOBS & FAKE DIAMONDS

I am way too practical ever to waste money on diamonds. Don't get me wrong, I think they are pretty, but there is so much more I could do with the money, like add more Japanese maples to the landscaping around my house. I told you I was practical. Besides, if I had an extra eight thousand dollars, I'd buy my dream Quarter Horse from Atwood Ranch, not a diamond.

In 2003, I co-chaired a fundraiser for abused children and raised over $400,000 for three social service agencies. In this role, I had to come up with a theme for the black-tie event. For the past twenty-one years, the event's logo had been a silhouette of a couple dancing in period clothing, parasol and all. Wanting the event to be a festive occasion that people wouldn't soon forget, I chose *Celebrate with a Caring Heart* as our theme, for which there was to be a new logo: tango dancers in ballroom attire dipping at the end of a dance. Trust Kate to put her oar in, however.

Privately, in the back of my mind, I came up with another theme for the evening, as well. It was "Real Boobs & Fake Diamonds," since a majority of the women attending the ball were sure to have just the opposite. Kate came right out in me, and suggested that theme to a few committee members, but the only person who laughed was my Aunt Linda. She got it.

At one of the Steering Committee meetings for the ball, I wore a beautiful pair of pretend three-carat pink diamond earrings. The Director of one of the agencies asked me if the earrings were real. I said they'd better be for twenty-five dollars.

That's my relationship with cubic zirconium in a nutshell. I'm too embarrassed to wear real diamonds, therefore I tell the truth to astonished admirers. They tell me "You're *not* supposed to tell the truth." So there! It's a problem!

The only fib I like to tell is about my "boyfriend ring". I love to buy beautiful zirconium jewelry for occasions such as the ball. My fantasy Prince Charming is the ornery movie star Ed Harris, who played astronaut Neil Armstrong in the aptly titled *The Right Stuff*. As a young child, I was always told that John Wayne was my mom's boyfriend. So why couldn't I have one of my own?

When I first displayed this gorgeous three-carat zirconium ring to my husband and kids, I explained that this was my Ed Harris boyfriend ring. They know me well enough to know that Ed Harris is not really my boyfriend. I figured, the diamond was fake, why not the story. Besides, *everyone* needs a wet-dream hero.

THE BOWLING-BALL FACTOR

I have always been attracted to balding men. Maybe God gave them hair loss to show off the good head on their shoulders. Besides, if it's the male hormone that causes hair loss, doesn't that make them virile?! I think so.

Oh, did I mention that my mom is way cool? When I was a junior in high school, she let me cut classes for a day so my boyfriend and I could go downhill skiing. It was powder conditions up at Mt. Hood (a rarity) and the sky was blue (another rarity in Oregon).

My boyfriend Luke was my first "Love of My Life." We dated for over two years and had a wonderful time together. On this gorgeous day we were so excited to go skiing together. Cuddling on the chair-lift up the mountain, I admired his receding hairline. I said to him "I'll still love you when you are completely bald." Luke replied "You're fat and I still love you." Ouch! That struck a nerve. Hey, wait a minute; I weighed a hundred and twenty-four pounds at the time. It's a good thing I didn't marry him.

I accidentally got even with him that very afternoon. We unpacked our picnic out on a snowfield away from the lift-lines. The weather was breath-taking; I swear I could see California! Along with our picnic we'd packed a couple of beers and proceeded to drink them. We ended up taking a long "nap" right there on the mountain top. Luke's buns got so sunburned he couldn't sit down for a week. Ouch! Sorry Mom! Hello...eggshells in my scrambled eggs.

STUD MUFFIN

Shortly after I moved to San Francisco and joined the Dolphin Club in 1991, I met Matthew, a cute young man, a couple of years my junior. He had patches of hair missing on his head and I assumed he was going through chemo.

Matthew and I enjoyed swimming in Aquatic Park together and we were nearly always at the same pace in the water. Eventually, on our first actual date, he explained to me that he had a condition called alopecia areata. It was something that had haunted him his entire life. At random, patches of hair would fall out and it would take months, or years to fully grow back. The emotional pain he suffered was visible and excruciating. A few weeks later, I suggested he "grab the bull by its horns," and shave his head.

The very next day, Matthew let me do the honors and shave his head. I was so nervous, worried that I would hurt him, that my hands shook. Fortunately no damage was done. His transformation began almost immediately. It was like seeing a new person emerge from a dormant cocoon. Going bald intentionally gave him a new self-confidence. It allowed him, for the first time in his life, to take control of his condition.

The fact is Matthew had a beautifully-shaped head to display. He grew a mustache that made him even more handsome. He quit his job selling carpet and trained to become a Paramedic. It was amazing for me to see him "hatch". Of course, he dropped me like a hot potato, but that was okay. I was so proud of him for morphing into this stud muffin! I was busy training for my English Channel swim and would be leaving for Dover soon anyway. We parted as friends, each of us going confidently towards our big adventure.

Deep down, Kate was always part of my childhood, like the time she poured glitter on my sister's wet hair when I was four years old. Now as an adult, I admire with confidence the mischievous but nice Kate inside me. I hope by the time I'm one hundred and four years old, just like my grandmother, I'll be all Kate. Talk about ornery: watch out great-great-grandchildren!

Do you own anything expensive, like diamond jewelry that you don't really care that much about?

Have you ever considered selling it to buy something you really value? What would you buy instead?

Describe your wet-dream hero!

Have you ever experienced the pleasure of helping others feel better about themselves?

"Happiness is an inside job."

—H. Jackson Brown, Jr.

I Dropped My Oar 14

It was late fall of 2007 and I needed to start thinking about the holiday season. I was overwhelmed with all the tasks at hand. The short list of those tasks included keeping up with the children's sport schedules, running the Portland Garden Club Market Basket's Fetch & Carry, (a holding station for customers to put their goods down while they continue shopping) working with the horses, maintaining a functional home, laundry, grocery shopping, and buying Christmas presents. The last thing on my list of priority was my self-worth, exercise, and diet. I turned to the bottle to help me cope with my frustrations.

I usually waited for the 5:00 p.m. news to start, when the cocktail hour officially arrived. Out came the gin and tonics, to soothe the emotional overload. Knowing my husband was at his favorite "tree house," The University Club, drinking and smoking with the men, justified my diversion. This way I could be relaxed and cope with his intoxication when he arrived home for dinner.

My subconscious thoughts were, "I can handle anything as long as the liquor store is open." Tim and I were having "fun" together being at the same exhausted level.

I didn't even recognize myself when I looked at the mirror, which I usually tried to avoid. Putting on my swimsuit and passing a full-length mirror on my way to the 50-meter pool was a slap in the face to my subconscious. I absolutely denied knowing myself in the mirror. It was as if we had never met before. Like a New Yorker walking the street, I literally refused to make eye contact with the stranger in front of me. It wasn't a good feeling.

SINK OR SWIM

I knew my boat was sinking and something needed to change. I thought about a time in my life when my weight was not an issue. I was a freshman at the University of Arizona, sowing my oats and majoring in electives. I was very happy, healthy, and had a boyfriend who was very gifted in the love-making department. In fact, if he were a department store, he'd be Harrods!

I held on to my chastity for the first three months of our relationship, driving him absolutely nuts. I had romantic expectations for my first college relationship and I put demands on him such as studying at the library together, romantic dining experiences, attending the theater, and long hikes in the desert. Paul was a good sport about my requirements.

Eventually, we consummated our relationship. I had never experienced such a skilled, attentive, caring, athletic performance in my life. We were both young and fit...I'll leave it at that. It was right out of a Nora Roberts *clitorature* novel!

Limited by our dormitory surroundings and the Sigma Nu fraternity house, we opted to rent a small apartment for the month of April. Our roommates couldn't have been happier, for us, and for themselves!

It was a difficult task trying to learn the Quadratic Formula in bed with the most gifted lover on the planet. Luckily, he was a Civil Engineering student and could help me with my math. Since then, the only time I used the equation was to bet friends at Jake's Restaurant that I knew it. It did come in handy after all!

$$X = \frac{-b \pm \sqrt{b^2 - 4ac}}{2a}$$

In May of 1980, I got the devastating news that Paul was transferring to Virginia Tech in the fall. While he was in the shower I sat at his desk, and being nosy, I read a letter from his mother. My bubble popped, and my heart was broken. He explained he needed to take care of his aging grandmother who lived in Blacksburg, Virginia. We discussed our relationship, knowing that a long-distance romance was going to be a challenge for both of us.

When the semester ended, Paul and I flew from Tucson to Las Vegas to meet my father and brother who had a business meeting there. While we were in Las Vegas, May 18, 1990, Mount St. Helens erupted.

To make a long story even longer, we had phone sex for the next six months, and eventually went our separate ways. We did keep in touch for the next few years, while he traveled in the Navy. Periodically I received international post cards from him. Eventually, we both married other people and our lives went on.

GOOGLED A GHOST

As winter approached in 2007, desperately seeking some form of happiness, I looked up Paul's name on the internet. I sent him an innocent e-mail asking if this was the Paul who went to the University of Arizona. He immediately replied, saying that he thought of me often and of the good times we shared together.

Suddenly, I realized that I had a lot to live for and it wasn't necessary to go down with the sinking boat. Knowing I could only save myself by swimming to shore, I also realized that my husband, Tim, would need to do the same in order to save himself and our marriage.

A SUNNY FUTURE

My priorities shifted and now I could see the whole picture and a bright future. I started to make time to go for walks in my neighborhood and to swim twice a week at the local club. As I grew more aware of my emotions, I became a stronger person. I needed to take responsibility for my own happiness and not look for others to fulfill my needs; I am in control of myself, and I alone determine my self-worth. Prioritizing a healthy lifestyle made way for enormous emotional improvements.

Have you ever felt as though your life was spinning out of control?

What did you do to bring balance back into your life, or are you still struggling?

Have you ever used the internet to track down old friends and acquaintances, and if so, what motivated you, besides idle curiosity?

Have you ever actually contacted people from your past, and why?

Was the experience of reconnecting positive, or negative?

What time of your life would you label "the best of times", and why?

"Treasure the love you receive above all. It will survive long after your gold and good health have vanished."

—Og Mandino

Spalicious 15

Some people refuse spa treatments because they feel uncomfortable being touched by a stranger. I was one of them, but quickly got over my neurosis after pulling a muscle right before the Lake Berryessa two-mile swim in Napa Valley. Desperate at finding myself unable to rotate my shoulders for a complete crawl stroke, I did the only logical thing. I went to the Calistoga Spa for a massage.

Initially, I was very anxious about having a man I didn't know touch my body, but I soon realized that being nervous was going to make my massage experience not only less pleasant, but downright uncomfortable. Not being keen on pain, I forced myself to relax, and let the master do his work which he did, brilliantly. After explaining to me the source of the pain in my body, he worked me like a lump of clay, kneading my aches, pains and modesty away. At the end of our session, I walked out purring like a kitten, slithering like a boa constrictor, and greased like Duck Confit. Luckily, there was a chaise lounge for me to recuperate on before taking a cleansing shower. Massage rocked my world!

I'm Not a Pampered Poodle

I used to think that people who "did the Spa," were pampered poodles with two legs. That was, of course, before I had the pleasure of getting pampered myself! I realized that, in addition to the obvious physical benefits I was getting from my treatments, there were things happening that were far less tangible. I'm talking about the glorious emotional release and spiritual renewal I felt after each visit. I quickly became a spa disciple and, in so doing, came to the conclusion that I had to stop feeling guilty for treating my imperfect body so well. It was time to accept myself fully for who and what I was, cellulite and all. If I didn't, all that pampering was going to be a complete waste of money. I'm nothing if not practical: I opted to sit back, enjoy, and learn from my kneading therapy.

The Perfect Gift

To this day, I look forward to my Spa Days—days exclusively for me. Granted, even though one of my favorite local spas is just a couple blocks from our house, I don't get there as often as I make it to Starbucks. It's on special occasions, like my birthday, that I treat myself to the full-body experience. The only thing I regret when I'm horizontal and being kneaded and pummeled, is that I have let so much time go by since my last treatment. I also love to give gift certificates to friends I know will cherish the experience as much as I do. Sometimes, when my around-the-block spa offers a great sale, I round up my friends and we make a day of it: Spa first; lunch afterwards; friendship the whole time.

WRONG-SIDE-OF-BED DAY

Do you ever wake up in the morning and realize it's a *low* energy day? Maybe the cause is PMS, depressing weather, or a personal situation. What if you allowed time to treat yourself to a spa experience, even if you don't want to leave your house?

On the rare occasion I find myself in this frame of mind, I accept my feelings and escape reality by letting Calgon take me away…remember the old 1960's commercial? The first step is to take my phone off the receiver, allowing no interruptions. It's then time to close my bedroom and bathroom curtains and put lit candles near my mirrors to gently illuminate the room. Next, I draw a hot bath, adding my favorite *Mr. Bubble,* (another nod to the 60's.) Surrounded by quiet, I submerge my head until only my face is at the water's surface. The sound of water soothes my soul as I relax, transporting me to another place. Refreshing the hot water occasionally, I resist getting out of the tub until I sense that the precious feeling of buoyancy has returned to me once again. My hair wrapped in a towel, I slip into my favorite bathrobe and crawl into my warm bed for a deliciously long nap. Then I start my day all over, with a renewed sense of energy.

GOD'S PEDICURE

Another treatment that I enjoy spiritually, physically and emotionally, is going for long barefoot walks on the beach. Just steps from our condo retreat on the Oregon coast, the endless sound of the ocean waves is nothing short of intoxicating. I love it.

Walking on the beach with my shoes off, letting the brutally cold Pacific Ocean sweep over my feet, recalls the endorphin rush of my Dolphin Club days in San Francisco. Once again, I get the ice cream headache, accept the pain and surrender to the adrenaline rush. The glittering silica in the sand brings back childhood memories of walking in bright sunshine on sparkling sidewalks.

By-passing the intact, bigger sand dollars, I go on a treasure hunt for the elusive miniature ones. Smaller than a dime, they hide on the broken-shell scum-line of low tides and are very easy to miss. No sooner do I visualize the small round shape than they begin to appear, as if by magic! If I see young children combing the beach for their own treasures, I will often share these tiny and very fragile gifts of the sea. At some point, a miniature sand dollar may even make an appearance at the Seaside Flower Show, an event I look forward to every August. It's an opportunity not only to test my creative skills, but also to compete alongside my mother in a friendly, fun atmosphere. This special treasure finds its way along side my miniature flower arrangement, giving it scale.

One of my three-inch flower arrangements with miniature sand dollars in the Seaside Flower Show.

If you haven't walked on a beach in your bare feet lately, you are missing out on a wonderful experience! Find your way to the ocean, a river, or a deep lake. You'll never regret making time to feel the sand between your toes and the icy water lapping at your ankles.

CANYON RANCH IDEA

As a Christmas present to myself, in December of 2007, I received a Swedish massage from a skilled masseuse, trained in Eastern medicine and acupuncture. I mentioned how wonderful I thought it would be to escape from reality by going to a spa for a week, eating nothing but spa food and getting non-stop treatments. To my delight, she told me there are plenty of places eager to pamper me in this way. I could choose from great resorts in Mexico, Costa Rica, and Tucson, to name but a few. Having spent two and a half years in Tucson, I had forgotten about Canyon Ranch, which was still being built when I was at the university.

Just playing with the idea, I googled the resort when I got home. I researched the amenities at Canyon Ranch, and was astonished by all the different programs they offered. I gathered the information and filed it under "Some Day." Six weeks later, that "some day" was "Now"!

The deep relaxation I experience during massage is a source of spiritual renewal, the cold-water adrenalin rush, a way to reconnect with myself on a physical level, and the candle-lit bubble-bath is my way of recharging low emotional batteries.

What do you do to renew and refresh yourself on a regular basis?

Be creative! A massage makes a great birthday present to yourself! Find places to paddle more often! Stock up on candles and bubble bath!

Kate Cronin Haslach

"It is by forgiving that one is forgiven."
—Mother Teresa,
For the Brotherhood of Man

Canyon Ranch Experiences 16

After ten long years working with a large law firm in Portland, my husband was going to take a well-deserved three-month sabbatical in 2008. I asked him what he would like to do for himself during that time. We talked about a golf camp for him, or maybe a sailing adventure.

I told him, if it were I taking the sabbatical, I'd go straight to Canyon Ranch in Tucson and treat myself to a full ten days of spa treatments and rejuvenation. He thought about it and suggested I take myself on a sabbatical, as well! Less than thirty seconds later, I was online, booking one week of their Life Enhancement Program and three days of free time at Canyon Ranch. This was the first time in what was then a fifteen-year marriage that I was going to do something all by myself and just for myself. I'd gained fifty pounds since our wedding and was completely stressed out. I didn't even recognize myself in the mirror. Against my husband's wishes, I gave up being a Prozac "zombie" for my

New Year's resolution, even though it meant that I might act like a bitch. I needed to figure out why I held in so much anger. I had to come to terms with what might be a permanent postponement of my dream to return to northern California and, in the process, come to terms with myself.

RETURNING TO TUCSON

It had been twenty-six years since I last flew into Tucson. The University of Arizona college days were long over; this time I was going as a guest at one of America's finest resorts. In 1979, when I was living in Tucson, Canyon Ranch was just being built. Now it is one of the finest resorts of its kind in the country.

My plane landed in Tucson and I found the warmer climate instantly comforting. Of course, if you take off from Portland, Oregon in January, just seeing the sun is a pleasure!

It was a first for me, after collecting my luggage, to find a chauffer holding a large card with my name on it, ready to transport me, to my escape from reality. After fifteen years of putting everyone else ahead of me, it was a welcome breath of fresh air to be first. My practical self reminded me that it would be a colossal waste of money to allow myself to feel any guilt over this trip. On the contrary, I would relax, and learn to treat my body as if it were my best friend, something I'd never done before. After all, I was in Sabino Canyon Heaven!

SPA FOOD LURE

The allure of spa food was quickly confirmed. I was astonished when I sat down for my first meal with my fellow guests, and encountered a five-course luncheon menu! Seeing the puzzled looks on our faces, Molly, the dining-room captain, suggested we order something from each course. It didn't take me long to discover that delicious food needn't be fattening. Eating well is about quality, not quantity. "I'm going to like it here," I heard myself saying.

LIFE ENHANCEMENT PROGRAM

The motto of the Life Enhancement Program at Canyon Ranch is: "Experience it for a week...Live it for a lifetime" It is a seven day program filled with education about physical, mental, emotional and life-affirming spiritual growth. It was absolutely worth the money, and there hasn't been a day since I left Canyon Ranch that I haven't thought back to something I learned during my week-long odyssey in the Life Enhancement Program.

McKENZIE TREATMENT

Back in Portland, earlier that January, I had been diagnosed with arthritis and was devastated when the doctor told me I should only ride a bike or swim for exercise. My long walks on the beach would only exacerbate the condition of my left knee. I'd blown out my anterior cruciate ligament in a skiing accident eighteen years earlier. After repairing it with a portion of my hamstring, the surgeon told me that someday I could look forward to arthritis—a gift from the replacement surgery. I thought I'd go crazy if I couldn't take walks...come on now!

When I scheduled my time at Canyon Ranch, it was strongly suggested that I meet with Rob, a Registered Clinical Exercise Physiologist, and McKenzie Therapist, to discuss my newly-diagnosed condition.

I found Rob to be a charming Scot, with a no-nonsense attitude toward physical health. He asked me why I was here and

I explained my condition. Without missing a beat, he put me on notice, saying, "You are never to use the word 'arthritis' again. Let's let your knee tell us what is going on." After a battery of tests, he told me I had a restricted range of movement in my left knee, and asked if I would be willing to do some stretches for the next twenty-four hours and come back the next day to see if there was any improvement. That was a no-brainer.

The following day I met with Rob and repeated the same exercises. I was amazed to discover a seventy percent improvement in my mobility. If I kept up with the stretching exercises, I was free to take long walks!

This experience taught me to not believe everything doctors say. It's silly when you think about it. You go into a vitamin store and ask the "professional" if you need vitamins. You see a chiropractor and ask if you need alignment…crunch, crunch, and crunch. You go to a surgeon and ask if you need surgery…"Come on now, it's a business," Rob explained; I had consulted an orthopedist about my knee pain, he took x-rays, saw that I had inflammation and stiffness and Bingo, arthritis!

My "Aha!" Moment

I experienced so many life-altering moments at Canyon Ranch. It would take another book to tell you about all of them. However, there was another, besides my misdiagnosis of arthritis, which truly rocked my boat.

When I booked my activities at Canyon Ranch I decided to sample some unconventional therapy. I went to a clairvoyant reading, an astrology reading, a *Sex and Spirituality* seminar, and a meeting with Peggy, a behavior health therapist, for a "Look into Your Psyche" reading, using Mari Cards. (Go to www.mari-resources.com for more information.)

I walked into Peggy's office and knew right away that she and I shared the same passion for horses. I felt a spiritual connection. Her office was decorated in Southwestern style: woven Indian blankets, Western saddles and native artifacts. I was enlightened by the Mari reading, but I was inspired by Peggy's spiritual guidance.

The next day, Peggy came to the Life Enhancement Center to give a lecture entitled *Meditation for a Change*. I'd been eagerly awaiting her arrival, as I knew first-hand her strength in spiritual counseling. She told a story about a friend of hers who'd recently lost fifty pounds. When her friend realized that men treated her "differently" now that she was thin, she felt uncomfortable and proceeded to put all the weight back on. All of a sudden I felt tears welling up inside me. There I was, sitting in the second row of the classroom, unable to contain myself and not even realizing what had triggered my emotions. I sat there as tears poured out of my eyes throughout the whole lecture. My challenge was trying to keep the volume muted. Poor Peggy saw my raw emotion and was stunned, as she tried to maintain the focus of her lecture. I stayed in the classroom after the lecture, trying to recuperate from the emotional roller-coaster I'd just experienced. It was my "Aha!" moment and everyone at the Life Enhancement Program knew about it. All I knew was I needed to see a therapist!

That afternoon I met with Linda, a therapist on-site. What had surfaced during Peggy's lecture was the subconscious agreement I'd made with myself the day I got married. I had chosen to gain weight deliberately to make myself unattractive to the opposite sex, in order to keep my marriage intact, or so I thought. Linda pointed out that I'd recently gone off Prozac, that my libido was thawing, and it frightened me. She said I needed to treat my new sexual awakening as if it were a little girl and to be protective of those feelings. To this day, I cherish her suggestions and realize they were essential elements in my own journey toward self-acceptance.

MY SURPRISE!

I learned so much about myself that very special time at Canyon Ranch. Even though I ate three square meals, plus snacks every day, for ten days, I lost fourteen pounds on the scale and a thousand pounds of emotion.

The day I left Canyon Ranch I allowed myself to cry like a baby. I now understood the power of their motto:

"Experience it for a week…Live it for a lifetime"

How self-aware do you think you are?

Every choice we make means losing the chance to make others, often forever. Do you allow yourself to grieve your losses, and accept the consequences of your choices gracefully, or do you minimize them, even deny them?

When was the last time you experienced an "Aha!" moment, as you learned something new about yourself? Was it fairly recent, or are you overdue for another?

Are you willing to challenge yourself, to feel uncomfortable, even scared, by exposing yourself to new and unfamiliar situations?

If you are not fond of challenges, then treating yourself to a few days at a resort like Canyon Ranch is a very gentle and enjoyable way to ensure support and guidance on your journey towards self-acceptance.

How else might you go about removing yourself from your familiar environment? Where might you go? What might you do? Go for it!

"A kind heart is a fountain of gladness, making everything in its vicinity freshen into smiles.

—Washington Irving

My Love of Horses
17

My parents purchased an Irish Connemara pony for my oldest sister Melanie's ninth birthday. We named her Cricket's Dewdrop - "Crickie" for short. She was a stubborn little pony with quite the attitude: for example, she would come to a screeching halt before a fence, sending my sister flying, but we all loved her. Soon, there were five of us (Huck, the youngest was too young) taking English riding lessons at the local stables. My sister Melanie eventually graduated to Thoroughbred horses and became an accomplished Show Jumper.

I was the black sheep of the family, choosing Western riding instead of English. By age nine, I was fully consumed with swimming and riding. At that time, my mom left it up to me to decide which passion I would pursue. Swimming won out.

It wasn't until my daughter, Caroline, turned nine and my son Pete, turned seven that I got back on a horse. I'd asked them to choose a summer activity that we could enjoy together at the beach and they voted for riding lessons at a barn near our beach community. Pete, it turned out, was happier sitting on the barn's heavy equipment, but Caroline immediately took to riding

By the time we returned home at the end of the summer, my daughter was mesmerized by horses and I knew I needed to find a place for her to ride once we were back in town. My husband and I had given Caroline the chance to try any and all sports. Not a naturally competitive person, she disliked contact sports: her idea of soccer was to stay as far away from the ball as possible! We wished only for her to find her passion and clearly, it was horses.

ABBEY CREEK STABLES SANCTUARY

We checked out local barns in the Portland area and got on the waiting list for lessons. Out of frustration, I opened the telephone book, looked up horses, and quickly found a barn near our house. Caroline and I jumped in the car and drove the short distance to Abbey Creek Stables. It wasn't one of those hoity-toity barns with indoor plumbing that we'd seen before. There was something special about this place. We later agreed it had truly been a blessing to find Abbey Creek, because there we were introduced to an equestrian method known as Natural Horsemanship, and to owner Shelley. As far as you could see, there were beautiful horses happily grazing on lush green grass or running in the seemingly endless sprawling fields. There was a metaphysical energy I experienced every time I drove onto the property. To this day, I find it very healing.

Caroline and I both wound up taking lessons in Natural Horsemanship from Kat, a gifted instructor. We learned that Natural Horsemanship* is based on the study of horse behavior. Horses are prey animals and humans are predators and if humans will moderate their predatory behavior around horses, then horses will act less like prey animals. We learned to build a relationship of trust and confidence with horses on the ground before ever venturing onto a horse's back. Most of all, we learned how to gain a horse's respect by using the words of Pat Parelli "Love, Language, and Leadership," all on the ground. Working with horses using natural horsemanship is incredibly therapeutic for people because it requires the human being to be self-aware. You can't work successfully with horses until you recognize how your own behavior affects a prey animal. The horse reads and responds to everything you do: how loudly you talk; how fast you move, how nervous or how confident you are, how rough or how gentle, how considerate or how disrespectful and, however much you may be in denial, whether or not you are dishonest about any of theses things!

It brought tears to my eyes to see my daughter flourish amongst the horses. I only wished I had learned the skills and confidence Caroline was gaining, when I was her age. Moreover, finding Abbey Creek Stables was the best thing that ever happened to our relationship. My daughter, confident in her riding skills, helped me become a better person around horses. We spent hours at the barn together building relationships with our equine friends. Eventually, we leased Jeena, a spirited Arab Quarter Horse, for Caroline to ride.

Within a few weeks, we learned that our dear Shelley was in stage four Lymphoma and that she was battling for her life.

* Foot Note (To learn more about Parelli Natural Horsemanship and the amazing stories of Pat and Linda Parelli, please go to www.parelli.com.)

Nonetheless, she always greeted us with a big smile on her face, as if there was nothing going on. I could feel her positive energy with each hug she shared with everyone. It was obvious, being around Shelley, that she genuinely loved what she did and was living life at its most authentic. I knew Caroline and I were at a special, healing place. Shelley has been in remission for the past four years and is still living life to its fullest. I am so thankful to be a part of the Abbey Creek Stables community.

MY MID-LIFE CRISIS BOYFRIEND – SHAM

You know the old saying, "Be careful with whom you fall in love!" I had my mid-life crisis affair with an Arabian! One of Shelley's two horses, Sham was a four-year-old dapple-grey National Show Horse. Even though he was young, and green, with little time under the saddle, I was drawn to him as if by some magnetic force. Gradually learning to trust each other, we literally built our relationship from the ground up. What I love most about Sham is his ability to communicate through his eyes. He lets you know *exactly* what he is thinking, whether he's frightened, or hungry, or just needs a hug.

After two years spent playing with him on the ground, I finally gained enough confidence to climb on Sham's back. I learned fast that green + green = black & blue, or in my case, a broken ankle and a collection of the wildest bruises you can imagine. Even though we loved and trusted each other, he was still flighty. His registered name, Champagne Flight, should have given me my first clue. Even though I loved him unconditionally, I decided at that point I needed to find an older horse that would be safer for me to ride.

HEALING MY HEART WITH ZOTTY BEAR

Kat brought Little Miss Melony, a ten-year-old strawberry roan Tennessee Walker, to Abbey Creek Stables for a buyer. When the sale fell through, I took a closer look at her personality. Minnie, as she was known, was as sweet as could be, as long as she got her way. I knew if I were to buy her, we would have to start Natural Horsemanship from the ground up. It would be good for both of us to start fresh, at ground-zero learning step by step the process of building respect for one another. I had never seen a strawberry roan horse with a flaxen mane and tail before, and I loved to watch this beautiful pink animal with the butterscotch mane and tail running around the pastures. She was gorgeous. I just didn't think that "Minnie" suited her.

Zotty Bear and I, on our summer vacation at Weston Stables in Surf Pines, Oregon, near the coast.

I got my first German Steiff Zotty Bear for my second Christmas. We were inseparable, and I used to carry him around the house as if we were attached at the hip. Each year, my collection of Steiff teddy bears grew. It seemed very natural to me, a child in a large family, that I should have my *own* family, of bears. Skipping Barbie dolls, I dressed up my bear family. I grew up with an empty suitcase under my bed. If the house ever caught on fire, I could put my precious bears in the suitcase and throw them out the window. Family first. To the day I went off to college, those bears lived on my bed.

My bear family

When I got ready to go to the University of Arizona, I wanted a safe place to store my bear family. My parents divorced while I was in high school, and I knew my mom would be selling the house while I was away. I carefully packed my bears in a cardboard box and gave them to my dad for safe-keeping in his garage attic. I never saw them again. My father remarried, and remodeled his house, and my bears were lost in transition. To this day, I don't know what happened to them, but it left a huge hole in my heart. For years, I couldn't even say the name "Zotty Bear" without bringing tears to my eyes. I changed *Minnie's* name to *Zotty Bear*. Now I get a big smile on my face whenever I say "Zotty

Bear". She brings so much unconditional love to my life; I don't know how I ever got along without her.

Six months after I bought Zotty Bear, Shelley called me up and asked if I wanted to buy Sham for my daughter Caroline. Shelley had seen what an accomplished rider Caroline had become and knew that she would have no regrets pairing those two up. My life was complete!

LIFE LESSONS FROM HORSES

So many of the life lessons I have learned from horses, I'm sure can be learned from any animal, be it ferret, cat, dog, or bird. Through my relationship with my horses I have become a better human being. I love learning to communicate with horses through body language, theirs and mine. They give me unconditional love every day of my life. When I am with them, my life is in harmony. Sometimes, instead of taking them from pasture to arena to play, I'll just sit on a log out in the grass field and watch them play with the other horses. They approach me for a hug and a kiss and to ask what we're going to do today. I reply, "Just *love*". Being around them is like being in a time-warp. I am so absorbed, I lose track of time. When I leave the house I say to my husband, "I'll be back by three, give or take a couple of hours!"

Horses live in the present. It's not about what happened yesterday or what's going to happen tomorrow. I have learned to set aside my problems in order to be with them, physically and mentally, in the now. I love the experience of present-tense living.

One of the most interesting things I've learned watching Caroline live and grow with her horse is that for both of them, being assertive is a blessing, a quality both needed to learn. It is the kind of assertiveness I wish I had learned at an early age. Today I see my daughter thriving in her relationships with both Zotty and Sham. Long since out of her shell, Caroline has become a confident, beautiful young woman, with an insatiable appetite for all things equine. I don't worry about her future; she has a great head on her shoulders and she is following her heart. She has three passions in her life: Sham, Zotty Bear and Michael Phelps!

I don't plan to be a competitor in the equine world. If my daughter should decide to go down that trail I will, of course, support her. For me, it is sufficient that I treasure the relationships I have with my horses and hope never to stop learning from them. My long-term goal is to volunteer at the Atwood Ranch Quarter Horse Breeding Program in Orland, California, helping foals imprint with humans at birth using the principals of Parelli Natural Horsemanship as their foundation. Even if it meant just grooming the mares and their foals, or cleaning out their stalls, I would still love to experience that environment. And who knows, I might have another affair, with a Quarter Horse this time, because there will always be room in my heart for more horses.

Zotty Bear stealing hay from Sham.

My Favorite Cowboy Sayings

My two favorite Cowboy Sayings that I know are true are: "Old cowboys never die, they just smell that way" and, "Dog may be a man's best friend, but a woman's heart is not complete without a horse."

If you have ever enjoyed a close relationship with an animal, you already know how that relationship connects us to nature and to our spiritual selves. The relationship between horses and human in particular is unique, based as it is on the trust placed in a predator by a prey animal. Horses have been used extremely successfully as therapy animals.

Have you ever spent time around horses, learning how to interact with them? If you are interested in finding out how therapeutic working with horses can be, I recommend a session with a teacher trained in Natural Horsemanship.

"Grow old along with me!
The best is yet to be,
The last of life, for which the first was made."
—Robert Browning, *Rabbi Ben Ezra*

Staying Grounded

I am by no means perfect, nor do I choose to be. I prevent my children from ever putting me on any kind of pedestal. You see, I did that to my father when I was growing up. I idolized him and thought he could do no wrong. When I was a teenager trying to survive my parent's divorce, my father came crashing down off the pedestal I put him on, head first. Trying to avoid that happening to my two children, I remind them that I have my shortcomings, as do they.

A SCENTED ROSE WITH THORNS

Today, I understand that in order for me ever to accept any part of me, I have to acknowledge all of myself, no holds barred. Like a beautifully scented rose, the package includes both thorns and special gifts. I choose never to become a long-stemmed rose, stripped of its thorns and its fragrance, grown in a foreign sweatshop greenhouse for mass-production. I am more of a species rose, one of those roses found in nature, known for their simple beauty, fragrance, and hardiness, not to mention their colorful hips!

So, speaking of thorns, there's my temper, which from time to time needs a dimmer switch. Early on, my mother recognized that swimming was a great way for me to defuse my short wiring. To this day, my children will remind me that I need to go for a swim when I am short with them.

My mother loves to tell the stories of what have become the legendary temper tantrums I threw as a three-year-old. If I didn't get my way, or people wouldn't pay attention to me, I'd hold my breath until I lost consciousness. Sure I was having epileptic seizures, my mom finally took me to a pediatrician. The doctor gave me a battery of tests and concluded I was a *brat*. He told my mother she should just ignore my behavior and walk away from me when I went into tantrum mode. Unfortunately for my mom, I'd reserve my particularly colorful fits for when my parents had guests over. There I'd be, at the top of the staircase. It sounds like something from *The Exorcist*! No wonder my nickname growing up was Mrs. Troubles. I remember Mother waving her finger at me, saying "You deserve a child just like yourself." Thank goodness Caroline and Pete fell off the tree and kept rolling. They're great apples.

Another thorn I have to work with on a daily basis is that I swear like a hockey player and have done so my entire life. There are two days a year I don't use curse words—New Year's Day, and the first day of Lent. After that I'll be damned if I'm not back at it. My swearing is like a geyser releasing steam from my brain.

When I was six years old, my father had me write down all the swear words I knew and put a check by them every time I said them. I think he found my spelling and check-list entertaining. I did spell one word correct, thanks to Woodstock. He recently gave me back the list of words he had kept in his scrapbook all these years, who knows why? Or why he gave it back to me. How the *hello* did I even know those words!

Okay. So those were some of the thorns. I promised myself never to mention them without also reminding myself of my gifts. Probably my greatest gift of all is the sense of buoyancy that permeates me, body and soul. It's my psychic buoyancy I'm most drawn to, however. That's the part of me that is mischievous, but kind, has a naughty sense of humor, and simply loves life. It's the part that keeps me going even when bumps in the road pop up. Most of all, it's the part that loves me, all of me.

Now, speaking of *all* of me, right now there are fifty extra pounds of me. My English Channel svelteness no longer exists. That said, I am committed to becoming fit and healthy by continuing yoga practice, meeting with Kimmie, my Ayurvedic Lifestyle coach, maintaining cardio work-outs, free weight training, and of course, swimming and walking. In writing this book, I feel as if I've lost a ton of internal baggage. Now I just need to let my Nabisco wetsuit (fat) shrink since I can now put my Garbinge eating in the recycle bin.

The point is, floating and buoyancy are about a lot more than how much you weigh. They exist in your innermost self, regardless of the pounds you do or do not carry. I now know that the true test of self-acceptance is loving and accepting every aspect of yourself.

EPIPHANY

Like a lot of my most important realizations, this one came to me while I was writing *this* chapter. "What," I wondered, "if all I really needed as a three-year-old was a hug from my parents?" Today, as an adult, I understand that they did the best job they could at the time and I don't fault either one of them. They were busy with their own lives, trying to raise six children. What I am saying, though, is that maybe the Kate inside me is that little girl fishing for acknowledgement and acceptance. Is that why I swam the English Channel? Is that why I am writing this book? Chances are, Kate is a permanent resident in my psyche. That's okay. Even though little Kate will probably always be looking for proof of approval from her parents, grown-up Kathryn knows that the most important approval comes from herself. This is my mantra today. Now I just have to live it! Living it means I acknowledge that both my parents love me even though they would not have taken the path I have chosen. And now as a parent, "living it" means that as I watch my own two children growing up, I want them to know I accept and approve of them. I may not always like some of the things they do, but I love them unconditionally and I hope, they will never have a little child inside them crying out for attention and love.

Watching Pete and Caroline grow up to be responsible young adults is one of the greatest pleasures of my life. And as I love them, they return that love on a daily basis. When I am upset, Pete gives me a huge bear hug and won't let go until I take a big breath and relax my tense muscles. And I do the same for him. We all need hugs from time to time. Caroline is my little optimist, who brings a smile to my face by reciting one of her heart-felt poems or by singing a song, and playing the keyboard or guitar for me. Whatever path they choose to take in the future, I will support and encourage them. I wish them the confidence to explore the wide world and to live life to its fullest.

The Nabisco Wetsuit

I know that for me, the challenge of self-acceptance is a life-long trip. Since that is so, I figure I might as well enjoy every second of it. Yes, I need, and I want, to lose the fifty pounds of insecurity that have grown under my skin, but if I can accept myself the way I am at this very moment, then I can begin to melt away the Nabisco wetsuit that has been insulating me all these years.

I will not lose weight just by accepting my overweight self, but by accepting the fact that I am not where I want to be, physically, right now, without allowing that fact to prevent me from taking action to reach my physical goal. I have learned that I am the sum total of all my thorns and gifts, and that my psychic buoyancy is what enables me to thrive in spite of the thorns.

Writing this book has been very therapeutic; it has brought many colorful emotions and much subconscious knowledge to the surface. Overall, it has strengthened my confidence in my ability to live a good life, without having to be perfect. I am ready to close the chapter in my life as an author and, drawing on the greater understanding of myself that writing this book has created, refocus my energy. This time, I intend to put into physical conditioning the same kind of energy that helped me train for my endurance swim.

My future is bright and I know in my heart that I will some-day return to the valley of grapes and to the city by the Bay. In the meantime, I am content to raise my children and live a buoyant life both as Kate and as Kathryn.

Let's have a little fun - get hold of a catalogue of roses and find yourself among the flowers. Are you exotic, hardy, old-fashioned, a hybrid? What color are you? How often do you bloom? Are you a climber, a miniature, or a shrub? Do you require lots of sunlight, or can you take a bit of shade? Do you have lots of thorns, or none at all? How fragrant are you, and is your scent spicy, floral, or fruity?

Take the metaphor as far as you like, and see what you learn about yourself in the process. If you're feeling especially bold, play it with a friend, and choose for each other!

Kate Cronin Haslach

If you are dissatisfied with yourself, body or soul, what simple, single, thing might you do today that would take you one step closer to satisfaction?

≈ 143 ≈

"A joy that's shared is a joy made double."
—Anonymous,
Recorded by John Ray, *English Proverbs*

Epilogue
Rock the Boat, Baby!

I believe *everything* happens for a reason. This belief helps me gain perspective when things don't turn out as planned. What can I learn from my experiences, whether they be successes, failures, or mere seconds of memory that have forever permeated my brain? I love flashbacks of the mustard in bloom in Napa Valley, of the setting sun creating an aura of light over the vineyards. The taste of saltwater entering my mouth and the pain of icy water chasing the blood to my heart is now but a memory. So too is the smell of cauterized blood during my skin cancer surgery. So it is that reflections on my life's moments both treasured and tortured, serve like a big picture-window, giving me a front-row view of my journey. As I look through that window, I can't help thinking about the "what if's?"

What if I hadn't swum on that particular day in 1992 and my toes had made their way to the beach of Calais, France? Would I consider my life any more meaningful because of that one incident?

Would it have made me a better person? What if my "failure" actually saved me from some unforeseen path?

I am willing to accept responsibility for all the journeys I have chosen because if it weren't for each and every one of them, I wouldn't be who I am today. For example, never in a million years did I ever think of adding *author* to my resume. I did not write this book to seek fortune or fame. I wrote it because, after forty-eight years here on earth, I have finally found my voice. Listening to one another, my brain and my heart have at last learned to be friends. And it is by listening to them both that I have learned to be self-accepting.

At one time I was fighting depression. I'd lost my oars and my boat was sinking. Long since back on board, Prozac-free, I'm rocking my boat, and loving every second of it. I am the captain of my vessel and I have two strong oars that will some day take me to shore. In the meantime, I'm enjoying my buoyancy as the current sweeps me toward new and surprising destinations.

I may not get approval from my family by writing this book. I didn't allow other people's lack of faith to stop me dreaming of swimming the English Channel either. I'm listening to that inner voice telling me "Don't be afraid of failure, or of success, for that matter. Just tell your story." I have many hopes. Someday, I hope to walk down the street and have someone stop me to describe how, after reading my book, they went skinny-dipping for the first time in their life. Maybe someone walking along the beach will take their shoes off and experience an endorphin rush from the cold water. Maybe someone will start a cooking club that changes their awareness of how much influence they have on their own life. Or better yet, maybe someone who followed their heart literally told their story, not worrying about the success or failure of their poem, song, book, or dance. Maybe you will be one of those people?

We all have dreams. You have yours. I have mine. I think about the one thing I can do right this very second that will take me one step closer to bringing my dreams to fruition.

One particular dream I have would be for Oprah to read these words, because she lives in my heart. I want her to realize what a gift she is to this planet, irrelevant of her waist size. She has enough heart to fill her body, and the strength to move mountains. I am proud of her. I want her to know that we can and need to accept ourselves at every part of our journey.

There will be people I already know and others I will never meet who may judge me because of my experiences or my appearance. That will not change me. I am who I am, gray hair, imperfect figure, with a huge smile on my face. There might even be insults from the mantourage sitting on their couches, about *Fat Chicks Float Well*. Oh well, I'm not running for President of the United States, or Miss America.

I'm accepting the journey called *life* with open arms and an open heart. That's the ultimate gift of buoyancy. I am so glad you joined me for this part of my trip, and I hope my story has helped to take you, personally, one step closer to fully accepting yourself and your own precious buoyancy.

☀

If you weren't afraid of success or failure, what would be your biggest dream?

Besides coming to terms with yourself here and now, what practical steps might you take towards making your dream a reality?

Acknowledgements

≈

I believe that our success in this life is largely determined by the company we keep. I want to thank everyone who has helped me along the way, especially the following people:

My husband Tim, daughter Caroline, and son Pete, for reminding me that it really is a big deal to write a book. Thank you for your patience, love and support while I escaped reality to step back in time.

To my friend and "grammar guru" Helen Kimmelfield; many thanks for your attention to detail and objective thought. Your "golden pencil" is a gift to my writing.

Dr. Lynda Falkenstein, thank you for giving me the motivation to get this book started.

Anita Jones took my words and turned them into a lovely book. Thank you for your creativity and expertise in book formatting.

To Mark London, John Skelly, and Jennifer Sliker of 500 Lbs., my appreciation for the use of your talents in creating my website, katehaslach.com.

To my sister Melanie Cronin Callander, and my mother Susan Schiffer, for their patience while reading my original chapters and their help in shaping the book.

To Gail Bowen McCormick, my mentor and friend, for the countless hours she supported me, in and out of the water.

To my friends Karen Maletis Graves, Shelley Smith and Shelley Rayhawk, who took time out of their busy lives to read my book and write comments for it.

Last but not least, to my therapist, Beverly Duke-Young for giving me the emotional support I needed, from the beginning to the end of the entire project.

Contact Information:
Kate Cronin Haslach
Fat Chicks Float Well, LLC
2065 NW Miller Road, #206
Portland, OR 97229

E-mail: kate@katehaslach.com
Website: www.katehaslach.com